Life
BUILDERS

ADULT GROUP
BIBLE STUDY

GW01071840

LEARNING TO TRUST GOD

WES HAYSTEAD

Gospel Light

Gospel Light is an evangelical Christian publisher dedicated to serving the local church. We believe God's vision for Gospel Light is to provide church leaders with biblical, user-friendly materials that will help them evangelize, disciple and minister to children, youth and families.

We hope this Gospel Light resource will help you discover biblical truth for your own life and help you minister to adults. God bless you in your work.

For a free catalog from Gospel Light please contact your Christian supplier or call 1-800-4-GOSPEL.

PUBLISHING STAFF
William T. Greig, Publisher
Dr. Elmer L. Towns, Senior Consulting Publisher
Dr. Gary S. Greig, Senior Consulting Editor
Larry Keefauver, Editor
Jean Daly, Managing Editor
Pam Weston, Editorial Assistant
Kyle Duncan, Associate Publisher
Bayard Taylor, M.Div., Editor, Theological and Biblical Issues
Debi Thayer, Designer

ISBN 0-8307-1825-7

How to Make Clean Copies from This Book

You may make copies of portions of this book with a clean conscience if:

- you (or someone in your organization) are the original purchaser;

- you are using the copies you make for a noncommercial purpose (such as teaching or promoting your ministry) within your church or organization;

- you follow the instructions provided in this book.

However, it is ILLEGAL for you to make copies if:

- you are using the material to promote, advertise or sell a product or service other than for ministry fund-raising;

- you are using the material in or on a product for sale;

- you or your organization are **not** the original purchaser of this book.

By following these guidelines you help us keep our products affordable.

Thank you,

Gospel Light

Contents

How to Use *Learning to Trust God*

This very practical study on *Learning to Trust God* has been designed to fit a variety of learning situations:

- You have a choice of course length (5 to 10 sessions).
- You have a choice of session time lengths (from 60 to 90 minutes).
- You have a choice of settings (classroom or home).
- You have a choice of meeting plans (as part of Vacation Bible School, or Sunday mornings, Sunday evenings, weekdays or evenings) and frequency (once a week, every day or night, weekend retreat).

Whenever or wherever you can get a group of adults together to explore their interest in and concerns about faith—this manual will be an invaluable guide.

This Leader's Guide

This leader's guide is a unique resource, offering a stimulating and enjoyable opportunity for group study or successfully teaching adults about God.

This leader's guide is unique because it...

- Offers the flexibility of completing this study in from five to ten sessions;
- Is based on the premise that a study of faith is a truly exciting adventure with great value for both long-term Christians and new believers;
- Explores sound principles of a balanced, healthy Christian life, encouraging people to apply their faith to their everyday lives;
- Provides useful handles for helping participants see the personal implications of the principles studied;
- Includes proven strategies for enjoyable group interaction, enabling participants to learn from the experiences and insights of others;
- Requires very few additional supplies for class sessions: An overhead projector is helpful, but not necessary. Blank paper, index cards, pencils and felt-tip pens are typical of the easily secured materials which help add variety and stimulate involvement. Suggested supplies are listed at the beginning of each session;
- Suggests practical actions participants can take to implement each session's learning.

Session Plan

Lessons are flexibly designed to be completed in one of three major time schedules:

- Option A—Sessions of 60 to 75 minutes each.
- Option B—Sessions of more than 75 minutes each.
- Option C—Two sessions each about 60 minutes, extending the series from five to ten sessions.

Two important symbols are used in the session plans to aid in extending the lessons over two separate sessions.

1. This symbol indicates the **two-meeting track** which allows you to extend lessons over two meetings each, giving group members more time for discussion about the practical application of that session's topic. The stop-and-go sign means to **END** your first meeting and **BEGIN** your second meeting at the point where the symbol appears in the session plan. Each of the lessons in this manual can thus be easily made into two complete sessions, for a total of ten sessions (Option C).

2. You will find instructions placed in boxes and marked with this clock symbol. This information provides optional learning experiences to extend a session over two meetings or to accommodate a session longer than 60 to 75 minutes (Options B or C).

Sample Session Plan

Getting Started

(10 Minutes)

Each lesson begins with a choice of two relationship-building, experience-sharing activities which also help group members begin thinking of the main truth of the session.

Getting Started Option

This option will add 10 minutes to the Getting Started section, either reviewing highlights of the previous session or further introducing the current session.

# Getting into the Word

(40 Minutes)

Each lesson contains three to five major points, enabling class members to explore several issues and the implications for personal application. For example:

Step 1—First Point (15 Minutes)

Complete instructions are given to enable the teacher to guide class members in helpful and enjoyable learning experiences.

Option

This option will add five minutes to the Step 1 section.

These optional activities explore aspects of each main point which could not be addressed in the shorter time schedules.

Note: If you are completing this session in one meeting, ignore this break and continue with the next Step.

Two-Meeting Track: If you want to spread a session over two meetings, **STOP** here and close in prayer. Inform group members of the content to be covered in your next meeting.

Start Option (10 Minutes)

Begin your second meeting of a lesson by reviewing the main ideas from the first half of the session. (Suggested review activities are in each session.)

Getting Personal

(10 Minutes)

Each session concludes with instruction and questions for summarizing session highlights, helping participants make personal application of a main idea, with suggestions for implementing the ideas in practical ways.

Getting Personal Option

This option adds five minutes to Getting Personal, probing one personal issue studied.

A Few Teaching Tips

1. Keep it Simple. This is not a study in all the evidences for faith, nor an attempt to refute issues raised by skeptics. This is a study of the examples of real life people who faced situations in which faith in God made a big difference. Participants will remember and apply far more if you keep the focus on one issue at a time, seeking to keep your examples and explanations as brief and simple as possible.

2. Keep it Light. Some of the session introductory activities in this manual are fun! This is intentional. Many people who most need this course are intimidated by their lack of faith. Often there is fear that their doubts will be exposed. People who are intimidated and fearful are not ready to learn. The light-hearted approaches are devices to help people relax so they can learn efficiently.

3. Keep it Significant. Because the course has some light touches does not mean its content can be handled frivolously. Keep clearly in mind— and repeatedly emphasize with your class—that this course is dealing with the challenge of living daily in active dependence and trust in God. The insights gained in these sessions can make a big difference, not just in how people view the issue of faith, but in the way in which they apply their faith in dealing with difficult situations.

4. Keep it Interactive. The learning activities in this manual provide a variety of involving experiences, recognizing the various learning styles which will be present in any group of adults. While some of the activities may not fit your preferred teaching style, by using this varied path to learning, you make sure that those who learn differently than you do will also have their needs met. A common type of involvement is having people share some of their experiences, helping one another expand understandings of faith and considering the ways in which faith makes a difference in real life.

5. Keep it Prayerful. Both in your preparation and in each class session, pray earnestly that you and your class will be open to trusting God in all areas of your lives: spiritual, emotional, social, financial, etc.

To capture the interest of people in this course:

- Share some of your own experiences in trusting God and His Word. To succeed in leading this course, you do not need to be a "giant of the faith," one who has seen dramatic evidence of God's intervention in your life. Nor do you need to be free of any doubts or questions. You do need to be honest about some of your struggles in seeking to understand and/or apply faith.

- Point out that while societies and cultures change and many life experiences are different for people today than for any preceding generation, God's promise to be with His people has remained constant in all of human history. This course deals with people who faced situations which at first seem far removed from modern life, but which were in many ways similar to circumstances we still must face.
- Allow people to think and talk about their own experiences. Many adults struggle to believe, finding it difficult to recognize God's presence in their lives. This course recognizes there is great value in allowing people to be open and honest in expressing their struggles with doubt. Admission of a problem is the first step in making progress towards growth.

Faith: Trusting God's Control and Care

Session Keys

Key Verses

"Be strong and courageous. Do not be afraid or terrified because of them, for the Lord your God goes with you; he will never leave you nor forsake you." Deuteronomy 31:6

"The Lord is my strength and my song; he has become my salvation. He is my God, and I will praise him, my father's God, and I will exalt him." Exodus 15:2

Key Idea

Faith is acting on the conviction that God is in control and that He actively takes care of His own.

Biblical Basis

Exodus 3:1-6; 4:1-5; 12—15; 5:19—6:1; 8:20-24; 9:22-26; 10:12-17; Deuteronomy 31:6; 2 Chronicles 20:18-22; Psalm 20:7; 37:3-9; 78:5-7; Matthew 9:27-31; 17:14-21; Mark 11:23-27; John 14:1; 20:30,31; Romans 1:16,17; 3:22-28; 2 Corinthians 4:13-18; Hebrews 11:1-3; 12:1-3; James 2:14-18

Background

'Twas the night before class starts
and so every creature
was sleeping so soundly,
except this nervous teacher.

The lesson was ready,
but I tossed in my bed,
while visions of bored adults
coursed through my head.

'Twas the night before victory
and all through the camp
there was light from God's cloud,
no one needed a lamp.

Pharaoh's army was hindered
from launching attack,
and the Lord sent a strong east wind
to blow the sea back.

As the first day of a new adult series approaches, many teachers begin to envision all that might go wrong. It is hard not to dwell on *What if...?* questions: *What if the people are bored and I can't interest them? What if I do everything I planned and still have lots of time left? What if I get asked questions I can't answer? What if no one comes?*

Whether you are a first-time teacher of adults or an "old hand," whether you are teaching a group you know well or will be facing them for the first time, the approach of the first session of a new series is likely to stir up a mixture of contrasting feelings. Along with anticipation of learning, making new friends and opportunities to minister, there is likely to be an unsettling dose of anxiety, uncertainty, even bona fide fear.

When you are plagued with butterflies in your stomach, sweaty palms or nervous knees, remember the words of Moses to the terrified people being pursued by the Egyptian army: "'Do not be afraid. Stand firm and you will see the deliverance the Lord will bring you today'" (Exodus 14:13). Surely, if God was able to make a dry path for His people to pass through the Red Sea, He is able to make a way for you to serve Him through teaching His Word.

Think about your own specific experiences with fear and faith as you prepare to teach this series. Faith is not the absence of fear. It is acting on the conviction that God is in control and will take care of you. Faith is not an attitude or an idea. Faith is the courage to do what God has said because of trust in Him who will do what He has promised.

Preparation

- Provide blank name tags and felt-tip pens. Make a tag for yourself.
- On a table at the front of the room, provide materials for one of these Getting Started choices:
  - **Choice 1: Why Does God Allow...?**—Reproduce copies of the "Why Does God Allow...?" handout on page 22, providing one copy per person. Provide pens or pencils for those who need them. Have a chalkboard and chalk or an overhead projector, blank transparencies and markers ready.
  - **Choice 2: I Doubt It**—Make a transparency of the "I Doubt It" handout on page 23. Set up the overhead projector, focusing it on a screen or a light-colored wall. Cover the bottom instructions with a sheet of paper. Have a transparency pen ready.
- Reproduce copies of the "The Faith of Moses: Between the Pharaoh and the Wide Red Sea" handout on page 24, providing one copy per person.
- **Option: Faith Reminders**—Cut construction paper lengthwise into 6x18-inch strips—enough for each group of four or five to have two strips; felt-tip pens (one per group); and masking tape.
- Provide Bibles for participants who may not have them. (It is helpful to provide identical Bibles so that any participants who are not familiar with locating passages can easily be assisted by being given the page numbers along with the Scripture references.)

Session 1 at a Glance

SECTION	ONE-SESSION PLAN		TWO-SESSION PLAN	WHAT YOU'LL DO
Time Schedule	60 to 75 Minutes	More than 75 Minutes	60 Minutes (each session)	
Getting Started	10	10-20	20	Get Acquainted—Introduce topic of faith
Getting into the Word	40	60-75	40	
Step 1 Moses' Faith Saves Israel	10	20	20	Explore Bible narrative of Israel's escape from Egypt
Step 2 Moses' Reasons to Believe	10	20	20	Compare Moses' experiences with our own "faith journeys"
			Session 2 Start Option: 10	
Step 3 What the Bible Says About Faith	15	20	20	Discuss verses about faith
(Step 4 Option) Beating the Barriers to Belief	(10)	(10)	10	Identify tips for dealing with doubts and fears
Getting Personal	10	10-15	15	Pray for faith in dealing with problems

Session Plan

Leader's Choice

Two-Meeting Track: This session is designed to be completed in one 60- to 75-minute meeting. If you want to extend the session over two meetings and allow group members more time for discussion, **END** your first meeting and **BEGIN** your second meeting at the stop-and-go symbol in the session plan.

The boxes marked with the clock symbol provide optional learning experiences to extend this session over two meetings or to accommodate a session longer than 60 to 75 minutes.

Getting Started

(10 Minutes)

Choice 1—Why Does God Allow...?

Welcome group members as they arrive and suggest that they make and wear name tags.

Distribute copies of the "Why Does God Allow...?" handout. Encourage each group member to find a partner and work together to mark each item. When members have completed their pages, have them compare their answers with those of other pairs. Explain that each person may mark different columns because they are thinking of the answers of different people they know.

While group members talk, write on the chalkboard or blank transparency: "Why God Allows..." Just below that title, write three column headers: "Number," "Most Helpful" and "Least Helpful." Then number from 1 to 8 down the left side. At the same time, be ready to greet new arrivals and involve them in this activity.

Once most have marked their sheets and compared them with others, ask for a show of hands of those who marked at least one person who might give the first explanation: "God really doesn't care about individuals." Write the number in the "Number" column on line 1. Ask for a show of hands of those who marked that explanation as the most helpful when facing a crisis. Write that number in the "Most Helpful" column. Ask how many marked it as least helpful. Write that number in the third column. Continue similarly for each of the other explanations. Ask those who added the optional explanation (number 8) to share it with the class. Then invite volunteers to tell why they think certain explanations were marked as "Most Helpful" or "Least Helpful."

After group members have shared their responses and thoughts, lead into the study by saying: **We are beginning a study of faith in which we look at some examples of people who faced situations in which it was probably very difficult to trust God. We have begun by considering some different perspectives on difficult times in our lives. Probably everyone faces situations in which we wonder if God cares about or even knows about the struggles we face. My prayer is that each of these sessions will help us learn more about trusting God even when it seems we are alone.**

Lead a brief opening prayer, asking God's help in building our faith in Him.

Choice 2—I Doubt It

Welcome group members as they arrive and suggest that they make and wear name tags.

Place the "I Doubt It" transparency on the overhead projector, turn it on and call attention to the instructions on the top part of the screen. As participants mingle, be ready to greet new arrivals and involve them in this activity.

Give a signal to gain everyone's attention. Welcome members to this session. Then invite volunteers to tell about an incident in which someone told them about doubting. After several have shared, uncover the rest of the transparency and invite group members to tell reasons people tend to doubt. List these reasons on the transparency.

After people have shared some reasons, lead into this study by saying: **We are beginning a study of faith in which we look at some examples of people who faced situations in which it was probably very difficult to trust God. We have begun by considering the issue of doubt. Not only do we sometimes doubt other people, often with good reason, we also face times when we doubt God and His Word. My prayer is that each of these sessions will help us learn more about trusting God in spite of the doubts which all of us face.**

Lead a brief opening prayer, asking God's help in building our faith in Him.

Getting Started Option: Faith Sharing

This option will add 10 minutes to the Getting Started section and will help members continue to get to know each other while encouraging further thinking about faith.

Welcome group members as they arrive and suggest that they make and wear name tags.

After completing one of the Getting Started activities, say: **Before we focus on an example of trusting God in the face of great obstacles, we're going to take a few minutes to share with each other some of the very real experiences, both positive and negative, that we have had with faith in God.** Divide the class into groups of no more than four or five per group. Then instruct the group members to share with each other a time when trusting God was difficult for them. To help people feel free to share honestly, briefly tell about a time when you struggled to believe God. Then comment: **If living by faith were always easy and enjoyable, we wouldn't need this course. Nor would we need the many verses in Scripture which encourage us to have faith.**

Allow groups about five minutes to share, then invite participants to briefly tell of times when they did act on their faith in God. Again, share an incident from your own experience to set the tone, keeping your example simple enough that others will not be intimidated in trying to match a powerful exploit.

Getting into the Word

(40 Minutes)

Step 1—Moses' Faith Saves the Israelites (15 Minutes)

Introduce this segment by commenting: **In this series we'll be looking at some well-known Bible characters who faced situations in which it was difficult to trust God. The first person we'll consider is Moses.** Divide the class into at least five groups of no more than four or five per group. Distribute the "The Faith of Moses: Between the Pharaoh and the Wide Red Sea" handout to group members. Assign each group one of the five sections on the worksheet. They are to read the verses indicated and then work together to write a one-sentence summary of those verses. (If you have more than five groups, assign the same section to more than one group. If you have fewer than ten people, deal with one or more of the sections with the whole class, then assign the remaining sections to small groups.)

Allow groups four to six minutes to read and talk about their assigned verses and to write their one-sentence summaries. Then ask the person in each group who will have the next birthday to read aloud that group's summary sentence. Encourage people to write down the sentences as they are shared.

After someone from each group has responded, discuss the following questions:
What factors made it difficult for Moses and the people to trust God?
What actions did Moses take that showed he trusted God?
How might this story have ended if Moses had not trusted God?

Comment: **All the objective, tangible evidence indicated that Moses' situation was hopeless. Trapped between the sea and the enemy, with his own people on the verge of rebelling, Moses had nothing to go on except God's promise and his memory of what God had done in the past.**

Option: Praising God Before and After

This option will add five minutes to Step 1.

Divide the class into two sections. Instruct everyone in one half of the room to silently read Exodus 12:21-28, looking for how the people praised God before they were released from slavery. Instruct everyone on the other half of the room to silently read Exodus 15:1,2,11-13,17,18 to see how the people praised God after they crossed the Red Sea.

After a moment for everyone to read silently, ask for volunteers who read from Exodus 12:21-28 to share what they discovered about the people praising God (v. 27: "the people bowed down and worshiped"; v. 28: "The Israelites did just what the Lord commanded"). Next, ask volunteers who read Exodus 15:1,2,11-13,17,18 to share examples of praise from "The Song of Moses."

Ask: **How does praising God, before and after, demonstrate faith?** Accept responses, clarifying if necessary: We often think of faith as *preceding* something, an expectation or a hope that God will act. So, by worshiping and obeying God while still being held as slaves, the Israelites showed they were trusting God to deliver them. But faith is also demonstrated by the response *following* an experience. By praising God after crossing the Red Sea, Moses and the people showed they recognized that God was responsible for their deliverance. By praising God both before and after, we show our willingness to recognize that He is ultimately responsible for all that we need in our lives.

Step 2—Moses' Reasons to Believe (10 Minutes)

Comment: It is easy for us to find fault with the Israelites for their lack of faith. Yet, honesty should compel us to admit that we are probably more like them than like Moses, who seemingly did not waver in the face of overwhelming evidence that their situation was hopeless. Evidently, Moses remembered earlier experiences with God while the people could only see their immediate dilemma. To help us develop "eyes of faith" like Moses, let's take a few minutes to recall some of the reasons he had for placing his trust in God.

With members in the same small groups as Step 1, assign one or two of the following passages for each group to read. It is not necessary to assign all the passages.

- Exodus 3:1-6
- Exodus 4:1-5
- Exodus 5:19—6:1
- Exodus 8:20-24
- Exodus 9:22-26
- Exodus 10:12-17
- Exodus 12:12-13,29-32

Allow three or four minutes for everyone to read, then invite volunteers from each group to tell a reason from their assigned passage why Moses had trusted God by the Red Sea.

After class members have shared some of the incidents in which God had instructed Moses and then done what He had promised. Ask: **What are some reasons we have for trusting God today?** Accept responses from class members. Be prepared to share a reason you have learned to believe God and His Word. Invite others to share experiences which have strengthened their trust in God.

Option: Faith Reminders

This option will add five minutes to the Step 2 section.

With class members remaining in the same small groups, distribute two strips of colored paper and a felt-tip pen to each group. Instruct each group to write words or phrases of encouragement about trusting God on one strip. Suggest two or three samples to prime the pump: "Faith: Know Who You Believe"; "Trust Triumphs over

Troubles"; "Put Your Faith Where It Matters." As groups work, distribute pieces of masking tape for them to use in mounting their strips on the walls around the room. A group which finishes quickly can make another one (or use the second strip as a backup in case the first one doesn't turn out as good as they would like). Conclude the activity by having volunteers read aloud the words and phrases from the mounted strips.

Note: If you are completing this session in one meeting, ignore this break and continue with Step 3.

Two-Meeting Track: If you want to spread this session over two meetings, **STOP** here and close in prayer. Encourage people to look for additional reasons to trust God during the coming days. Inform group members that your next meeting will further explore what the Bible says about faith and ways to overcome the barriers that can block our belief.

Start Option: You've Just Gotta Believe (10 Minutes)

Welcome group members as they arrive and suggest that they make and wear name tags.

Begin your second meeting by inviting class members to share situations and experiences in which people express the value of some type of faith. Be prepared to share a few examples to stimulate thought and interaction. For example, athletes often talk about the need to have faith in themselves, their team or their coach. Ask: **What are some other circumstances in which you've heard someone stress the need to have confidence in someone or something?**

After several have shared, ask: **What value is there in a person believing or not believing that he or she will succeed?** Accept several responses, pointing out if necessary that in most activities, we tend to do better or try longer if we think success is possible.

Write across the top of the chalkboard or a blank overhead transparency the following three terms: "Wishful thinking," "Confidence," "Faith in God." Ask: **What do these terms have in common, and how are they different?** Invite several people who have not yet commented to share their reaction to the question.

Then continue with Step 3 and proceed through the remainder of the session.

Step 3—What the Bible Says About Faith (15 Minutes)

Introduce this segment by commenting: **We've spent a little time thinking about some of the values of believing in something. Now we're going to focus on the greater value of trusting in God. Let's take a look at some of the things the Bible tells us about having faith in God.**

Divide the class into groups of no more than four to six. Assign each group one or two of the following Scriptures. It is not necessary to assign all the passages. The groups are to read their verses, then discuss: **What does this passage teach me about faith?**

• 2 Chronicles 20:18-22

- Psalm 37:3-9
- Matthew 9:27-31
- Matthew 17:14-21
- Mark 11:23-27
- Romans 1:16,17
- Romans 3:22-28
- 2 Corinthians 4:13-18
- Hebrews 11:1-3; 12:1-3

Allow five minutes for the groups to read and talk, then instruct each group to take one more minute to agree on one key idea from their passages to share with the rest of the class. After the minute is up, ask each group to identify the person in their group who most recently had a haircut (or an ice cream cone, or out-of-town-company—any common experience that you can use to encourage participation from the full spectrum of your class members). That person is to report for his or her group.

Be prepared to add a sentence or two to clarify or focus understanding about what each passage is teaching. For example:

- 2 Chronicles 20:18-22 (Faith in God is expressed through songs of praise.)
- Psalm 37:3-9 (Faith in God involves trusting, delighting, committing and patiently waiting.)
- Matthew 9:27-31 (Faith in God brings benefits in proportion to that faith.)
- Matthew 17:14-21 (Even a small amount of faith in God brings great results.)
- Mark 11:23-27 (Faith in God puts no limits on God's power and goodness.)
- Romans 1:16,17 (Faith in God gives us God's power for salvation.)
- Romans 3:22-28 (Faith in God is the universal means of access to God's forgiveness.)
- 2 Corinthians 4:13-18 (Faith in God brings eternal life, even in the face of our own mortality.)
- Hebrews 11:1-3; 12:1-3 (Faith in God is certainty in Jesus' perfect provision for our salvation.)

Summarize this segment of the study by reminding class members: **The core issue about faith is not *how much* someone has, but *where* that faith is placed. Perfect faith directed toward anything that is imperfect will ultimately bring disappointment. But imperfect faith which is fixed on God's perfection will succeed.**

Option: Faith and Action

This option will add five minutes to the Step 3 section.

Read aloud James 2:14-18. Then ask: **What does this passage add to our understanding of faith?** Accept responses from class members. Then point out: **While James says it is possible for a person to *claim* to have faith without any deeds in support, he clearly does not say it is possible for a person to really have faith without deeds. This is not an argument for salvation by works. Instead, it is a powerful declaration that genuine faith must be more than an inner assent to truth. Real faith in Christ will produce good deeds which reflect the character of Christ.**

Alert the class that this issue will be explored more fully in a later session.

Step 4 Option—Beating the Barriers to Belief (10 Minutes)

Have class members return to the same small groups formed in Step 3 to share with each other the factors which have at times gotten in the way of their faith. To help them feel comfortable with this sharing, briefly mention one or two situations, people or attitudes which have hindered the growth of your faith.

Allow three or four minutes for groups to talk, then ask for volunteers to share one of the barriers mentioned and to suggest an idea for overcoming that obstacle. After several have responded, ask for volunteers to read the following verses and tell what each one suggests as a way to build up our faith:

- Psalm 20:7 (Thinking about the inadequacies of human resources helps us to recognize the superiority of trusting in God.)
- Psalm 78:5-7 (God's Word is crucial to the development of faith, not only for children, but for everyone.)
- John 14:1 (Trusting in God is an action we can choose to take. Even in the midst of circumstances which trouble our hearts, we can decide whether to put our trust in ourselves or in God.)
- John 20:30,31 (Faith must have a point, a purpose. It is not a vague, nebulous fantasy, but a specific assurance in Christ that brings everlasting life.)

Getting Personal

(10 Minutes)

Invite participants to suggest areas of life in which it is sometimes difficult to trust God. Be prepared to briefly share a personal circumstance in order to set a climate for honest interaction. As situations or problems are shared, list them on the board or a blank transparency.

After two or three minutes of sharing, ask everyone to privately select one or two items from the list which touch on an area of struggle they have faced. Then have class members share with their same small groups which item(s) they chose.

Instruct the groups to conclude their sharing by having each person pray for the person to his or her right, asking God to build the faith of that person in the circumstance mentioned.

Alert the groups that as they are praying, when there is one minute left, you will lead a brief prayer to summarize their concerns.

Getting Personal Option: I Believe, Therefore...

This option will add five minutes to the Getting Personal section.

Give class members up to two minutes in which to call out the truths that they believe about God. List these on the left side of the chalkboard or an overhead transparency. Leave space between each item listed.

After two minutes, refer to the items listed and invite volunteers to suggest practical actions that should be the result of such beliefs. Add these actions to the right side of the board or transparency. Members may suggest more than one action for specific beliefs. It is not necessary to write something about each belief. Just take enough time to clearly make the point that faith must lead to action.

Before participants leave announce: **Our next session will focus on recognizing God's presence, even when dealing with people and situations we would prefer to avoid.**

Why Does God Allow...?

| Disease? | Birth Defects? | Poverty? | Terrorist Bombings? |
| War? | Mental Illness? | Child Abuse? | Drive-By Shootings? |

Mark the box that indicates the explanation the following people would be most likely to give to explain how God can allow terrible things to happen to people:

	Your Coworker	Your Mother-in-Law	Your Neighbor	Your Pastor	You
1. "God really doesn't care about individuals."					
2. "God can't do anything about it. He's not really all-powerful."					
3. "God is punishing those people because they deserve it."					
4. "God has a long-term plan we can't see which makes some suffering necessary."					
5. "There is no God. At least not one that gets involved in our lives."					
6. "When people chose to sin, we ruined the perfect world God made and we all suffer the results."					
7. "God never promised bad things wouldn't happen to us. He promised to be with us no matter what."					
8. Other:					

Which of the above answers would you find most helpful when facing a crisis?

Least helpful?

Why?

I Doubt It

Welcome!

I Doubt It

Ask at least two people in the class to tell you about a time when they doubted what someone had told them. (They can change the names to protect the doubtful.)

Based on the stories you heard, what are some reasons people tend to doubt?

The Faith of Moses:

Between the Pharaoh and the Wide Red Sea

Write a one-sentence summary of your assigned section of this famous story.

The Purpose: Exodus 14:1-4

The Problem: Exodus 14:5-9

The People: Exodus 14:10-12

The Promise: Exodus 14:13-18

The Passage: Exodus 14:21-25

Faith: Recognizing God's Presence

Session Keys

Key Verses

"Trust in the LORD and do good; dwell in the land and enjoy safe pasture. Delight yourself in the LORD and he will give you the desires of your heart. Commit your way to the LORD; trust in him and he will do this: He will make your righteousness shine like the dawn, the justice of your cause like the noonday sun." Psalm 37:3-6

"Now faith is being sure of what we hope for and certain of what we do not see." Hebrews 11:1

Key Idea

Faith is strengthened by an awareness of God's powerful presence.

Biblical Basis

Numbers 22:21-31; Deuteronomy 30:19; 31:6; Joshua 24:15; 2 Kings 6:8-23; 7; Psalm 14:1-3; 34:7; 37:3-6; 91:11,12; 121:7,8; Proverbs 8:10; 16:16; Isaiah 26:3,4; 42:18-20; 64:6; Haggai 1:13; Matthew 5:44; 28:20; Luke 12:16-21; 24:13-16; John 7:17; 15:16

Background

> If you can keep your head
> when all about you
> are losing theirs,
> they may see something you haven't picked up on yet.

Numerous games we used to play in childhood involved sending one child out of the room while everyone else was let in on some "secret." When that child returned, the game began with the child who was "it" trying to guess what everyone else knew. Such games were usually fun, but they had an underlying tension, for no one likes being "in the dark" or being the last person to "catch on." Great feelings of insecurity are aroused whenever a person wonders: *Am I missing something here?*

Doubts about God's powerful presence in our lives cause far more serious problems. When we go about the business of living, unaware that God is with us, we miss out on seeing Him accomplish His purposes in our lives.

Just like in childhood games, we may have a vague sense that something is going on. We feel uneasy because we aren't certain that God is with us nor do we understand what He is doing. We often find it hard to pay attention to the evidences of God's presence. When we are especially under pressure, we tend not to see how God has already gifted us to meet life's current challenge.

In such situations, how do we "open our eyes" to better see Him at work in our lives? Just as Elisha prayed for his servant, we need to ask God to help us focus, listen and pay attention. Awareness of God's presence is not manufactured on our own. It is a gift from God whenever we ask. It is a gift, not for our own blessing, but to enable us to participate in God's purposes.

Preparation

- Provide blank name tags and felt-tip pens. Make a tag for yourself.
- On a table at the front of the room, provide materials for one of the following Getting Started choices:
  - **Choice 1: I Never Noticed**—Prepare four large sheets of newsprint or butcher paper, each with one of the following phrases written in large, bold letters: "I never noticed...," "Where did THAT come from?," "How could I miss...?," and "...right under my nose!" Mount each sheet on a different wall in your classroom.
  - **Choice 2: I Notice God When...**—Reproduce copies of "I Notice God When..." handout on page 36, providing one copy per person. Provide pencils or pens for those who need them.
- Have a chalkboard and chalk or a blank transparency, transparency pen and overhead projector ready.
- Write the following three questions on a blank transparency or poster:
  - What evidence does the passage give that your assigned character was or was not conscious of God's involvement in this situation?
  - Based on this evidence, describe what you think this character was depending on for success?
  - What difference do you think this awareness or lack of awareness of God's presence made in this character's attitudes and actions?
- Reproduce copies of "Becoming Alert to God's Presence" handout on page 37, providing one copy per person.
- Option: Is God Really with Us?—Have sheets of colorful construction paper, at least 9x12-inch (one sheet per group of up to six members), colored felt-tip pens and masking tape ready.
- Start Option: Hebrews 11:1—Locate four to six different New Testament translations. From each translation, copy Hebrews 11:1 on index cards, one word per card. Keep the cards for each different translation separate, mixing up the order of each set of cards. Have enough chocolate kisses to give one or two to everyone in the class.
- Provide Bibles for those who do not bring one.

Session 2 at a Glance

SECTION	ONE-SESSION PLAN		TWO-SESSION PLAN	WHAT YOU'LL DO
Time Schedule	60 to 75 Minutes	More than 75 Minutes	60 Minutes (each session)	
Getting Started	10	10-20	20	Get Acquainted—Introduce ways we miss what's obvious
Getting into the Word	40	60-75	40	
Step 1 Elisha Sees God's Army	10	20	20	Contrast points of view of characters
Step 2 Elisha Acts on His Faith	15	20	20 / Session 2 Start Option: 10	Analyze the basis for Elisha's surprising kindness
Step 3 Becoming Alert to God's Presence	15	20	20	Discuss ways to nurture awareness of God in daily life
(Step 4 Option) Making "Faith-Based" Choices	(10)	(10)	15	Consider implications of acting on faith
Getting Personal	10	10-15	15	Pray for responsiveness to God's presence

Session Plan

Leader's Choice

Two-Meeting Track: This session is designed to be completed in one 60- to 75-minute meeting. If you want to extend the session over two meetings and allow group members more time for discussion, **END** your first meeting and **BEGIN** your second meeting at the stop-and-go symbol in the session plan.

The boxes marked with the clock symbol provide optional learning experiences to extend this session over two meetings or to accommodate a session longer than 60 to 75 minutes.

Getting Started

(10 Minutes)

Choice 1—I Never Noticed

Welcome group members as they arrive and suggest they make and wear name tags.

Call attention to the sheets of paper mounted on the walls and invite group members to ask at least three other members to tell about a time they became aware of something that probably should have already been obvious to them. Share an example or two from your own experience ("I complimented my wife on her hairstyle and she told me she had changed it several days ago." "I struggled for hours with a new software program before I discovered a key instruction I had overlooked." "I knew my husband for several years before I realized he was the right man for me.").

After five or six minutes of group interaction, invite volunteers to share an interesting experience they heard someone else tell about. Then comment: **When someone is talking about a person who is woefully unaware of something obvious to everyone else, we often hear the expression, "He (or she) doesn't have a clue." As we have thought about times when we failed to notice something, it should be obvious that we all have times when we are clueless about something. This session will focus on our frequent lack of awareness of God's presence. Often we go about our business and struggle through problems without giving God more than a passing thought, if any. We're going to consider how to become more aware of God's direct involvement in our everyday lives.**

Choice 2—I Notice God When...

Welcome group members as they arrive and suggest they make and wear name tags.

Distribute copies of "I Notice God When..." and instruct members to take several minutes to list on their sheet the places and situations which tend to make them aware of God. Mention two or three items from your experience which have nudged you to think of God's involvement in your life.

After three or four minutes, invite volunteers to call out one item from their lists. List these on the chalkboard or an overhead transparency as group members mention them.

After several group members have responded, wrap up the discussion with a remark similar to this: **These moments of thinking about what has triggered our awareness of God's presence help to introduce this session's topic: Faith is being aware of God's presence. Perhaps it has already occurred to you that there may be significant stretches of time when, for all practical purposes, you are totally unaware of God's presence. This session will help us explore ways to nurture active faith which keeps us alert to God's involvement in our lives.**

Getting Started Option: People Who Didn't Notice—At First

This option will add 10 minutes to the Getting Started section.

After completing one of the Getting Started activities, say: **Before we look at a classic incident which contrasts awareness and lack of awareness of God's presence, let's look at several examples of people who simply did not "get it."** Divide class into five groups with no more than five or six per group. If the class is large, have more than one group do the same assignment. If the class is small, it is not necessary to assign each passage. Assign each group one passage to learn about people who were, at least for a time, unaware of God at work:

Group One—Numbers 22:21-31

Group Two—Psalm 14:1-3

Group Three—Isaiah 42:18-20

Group Four—Luke 12:16-21

Group Five—Luke 24:13-16

After several minutes, ask volunteers from the groups to share what they discovered about unawareness of God's presence. To encourage discussion, ask two or three questions, such as: **What contributed to this lack of awareness? What problems result from not being aware of God? What causes a person to change from being unaware to becoming more aware?**

It is not necessary at this point to fully resolve these questions. Simply seek to stimulate interest in further exploration.

Getting into the Word

(40 Minutes)

Step 1—Elisha Sees God's Army (10 Minutes)

Introduce this segment by commenting: **Sometimes we blame the fast pace of modern life for hindering our awareness of God's presence. People often yearn for a simpler, less hectic time, which would be more conducive to spiritual consciousness. However, the problem goes deeper than that since the Bible is full of stories of people in a simpler, slower-paced society who were oblivious to God's activity in their lives.**

With members in five (or more) groups of up to four to six per group, assign each group one of the following characters in 2 Kings 6:8-17: Elisha, Elisha's servant, the king of Aram (probably Ben-Hadad), the king of Israel (probably Joram), the officers and soldiers of Aram. **Listen as I read this story, then talk in your group about your assigned character's awareness of God's presence. Ask yourselves the following questions** (Show transparency or poster you prepared.)**:**

What evidence does the passage give that your assigned character was or was not conscious of God's involvement in this situation?

Based on this evidence, describe what you think the character was depending on for success.

What difference do you think this awareness or lack of awareness of God's presence made in this character's attitudes and actions?

Read the passage aloud (or select a class member who can read with expression). Allow two or three minutes for groups to talk about the questions, then call for volunteers to share their groups' responses.

After the group reports have been made, ask: **Based on this one incident, what do you see as determining the degree to which a person is aware of God's active presence?** (Obviously, the passage does not give a definitive answer, but the phrase used to identify Elisha—"man of God"—is a strong clue that a person must nourish an ongoing personal identification with God—a desire to be a person of God, in order to develop the ability to discern that God is near.

Option: Is God Really with Us?

This option will add 10 minutes to the Step 1 section.

Remaining in the same small groups as before, give each group a sheet of construction paper and one or two colored felt-tip pens. Assign each group one of the following verses that declare God's presence and assistance. It is not necessary to assign every verse. Instruct each group to copy the words of their passage on the paper as a reminder throughout the session of God's presence.

- Deuteronomy 31:6
- Psalm 34:7
- Psalm 91:11,12
- Psalm 121:7,8
- Isaiah 26:3,4
- Haggai 1:13
- Matthew 28:20

As the groups finish their verses, mount them on the walls around the room. Read the verses aloud.

Step 2—Elisha Acts on His Faith (15 Minutes)

Introduce this segment by asking: **Now that both Elisha and his servant were aware of God's army surrounding the enemy army, what possible actions might Elisha take now?** Ask group members to suggest ideas (ask God to destroy the enemy; ask God to help him escape from this entrapment; etc.), and list them on the left side of the chalkboard or a blank transparency.

Then ask a volunteer to read aloud 2 Kings 6:18. Ask: **Now that the enemy army is blind, what are Elisha's options?** Ask group members to suggest more ideas (escape, take their weapons, etc.), and list their ideas on the right side of the chalkboard or transparency.

Now ask another volunteer to read aloud 2 Kings 6:19-21. Point out that Samaria was the capital of Israel, and was located several miles from Dothan, the home of Elisha. Ask: **What reasons would the king of Israel have had for killing the enemy soldiers?** Accept suggestions from the group. (Obviously, this was an opportunity to strike a severe psychological and physical blow against the king of Aram.) **Based on your observations of human experience, how would most people evaluate such a strategy?** (Because these soldiers had been conducting raids into Israel's territory, a very high percentage would probably consider the king's plan justified and would expect it to be a deterrent to future raids. Based on a perspective that only considered the military/political/personal issues involved, it is easy to see how the king could look on this situation as a golden opportunity to get rid of some dangerous enemies.)

Read aloud 2 Kings 6:22,23. Ask: **What do you think was Elisha's basis for rejecting the king's plan and treating the enemy with kindness?** (In keeping with Elisha's behavior throughout the entire narrative, he continues to make decisions based on the conviction that God, not kings or armies, is truly in control. Obviously, the enemy army had not been captured by any power or brilliance on the part of Israel's leaders, but solely by God's intervention. Thus, Elisha's resolution shows his profound trust in God's care.)

Option: A Slow Learner

This option will add five minutes to the Step 2 section.

Invite participants to consider the temporary nature of the results of Elisha's faith. While the incident ends with the note that "the bands from Aram stopped raiding Israel's territory" (2 Kings 6:23), this was only a temporary lull. The next verse tells us that "Ben-Hadad king of Aram mobilized his entire army and marched up and laid siege to Samaria" (v. 24). The poor man just did not get it. In spite of the evidence of God's protection of Israel, he continued to act without regard to God's presence, with disastrous results (see 2 Kings 7).

Ask: **How many of you have ever seen evidence of God's presence in your life or that of someone close to you?** Then ask: **How many of us who raised our hands have ever at a later time forgotten to trust that God was with us in another situation?** Then comment: **When we are honest with ourselves, much of the time, we probably have more in common with the kings of Israel and Aram than we do with Elisha. In spite of the promises in Scripture and the evidence of our experiences, we still find it difficult to recognize that God is with us.**

Note: If you are completing this session in one meeting, ignore this break and continue with Step 3.

Two-Meeting Track: If you want to spread this session over two meetings, **STOP** here and close in prayer. Encourage participants to set aside time each day to praise God for being with them, and to confess their tendency to forget that He is near.

Start Option: Hebrews 11:1 (10 Minutes)

Welcome members as they arrive and suggest they make and wear name tags.

Begin your second meeting by arranging the chairs in four to six circles, placing the sets of the Hebrews 11:1 index cards you prepared face down in the center of the circles, one set per circle.

As class members arrive, have them divide evenly among the circles. Each person selects the top card from that stack without looking at any of the remaining cards or showing his or her word to anyone in another circle.

As the first few class members arrive, make sure that at least two of them join each circle, so no one is sitting alone. Once you decide it's time to start (either half of the chairs are filled, or the "official" starting time has arrived) instruct people to take turns selecting the remaining cards in their stacks, then work together to put their cards together into a sentence. If groups get stuck, tell them to look up Hebrews 11:1, alerting them that their cards might not match exactly, since you used different translations. When the first group completes the verse, announce, "We've got a winner!" As each group finishes, announce, "We've got another winner!" When all groups are finished, distribute chocolate kisses to everyone.

As groups are enjoying their prize, comment that Hebrews 11:1 is probably the most famous verse in the Bible about faith. Each group completed a slightly different wording for the verse to help the class focus in fresh ways on these familiar words. Have one group at a time read the words of Hebrews 11:1 in unison.

Then continue with Step 3 and conclude the session.

Step 3—Becoming Alert to God's Presence (15 Minutes)

To help people think about how to become aware of God in the middle of everyday life, distribute the "Becoming Alert to God's Presence" handout, plus pens or pencils to those who need them. Point out: **The words in boldface type call us to specific actions and attitudes necessary to receive God's promises. Each statement of what we are to do is repeated on the page. Choose one or two of the phrases and write a description of at least two specific ways you can put each action or attitude into practice in daily life.** Share two or three examples of your own to help people get started.

After three or four minutes, invite class members to form groups of two or three and share with each other one or two of the actions they wrote down. After several minutes of sharing, lead the class through the phrases on the handout page, inviting volunteers to share what they wrote for each one. Be prepared to share additional examples or insights.

There are at least three themes presented in these verses:

• **Spiritual and Practical**

The phrases "trust in the Lord" (used twice for emphasis), "delight yourself in the Lord" and "commit your way to the Lord" indicate the importance of emphasizing the spiritual dimension of life—the essential requirement of actively seeking God. At the same time, the phrases "do good," "dwell in the land" and "enjoy safe pasture" evoke awareness of the practical, day-to-day things we do. The spiritual and practical are not shown as contrasts, but as interwoven aspects of life. We clearly see how the spiritual links to the practical and the practical influences the spiritual in the phrase "commit your way to the Lord." The term "your way" refers to the totality of a person's life: schedule, goals, work, values, play, family. Thus, the foundation of developing an awareness of God's presence is to intentionally, as an act of faithful submission, entrust every dimension of life to God's ultimate control.

- **Action and Attitude**

  Words like "do good" and "dwell" refer to tangible, physical things we do. Words like "trust," "enjoy" and "delight" bring in our emotional, inner elements. Many people focus their time and energies mainly on the "inner life." Many others focus on acts of obedience. To fully interact with God's person and presence, we must open both areas of life to Him.

- **Dependence and Appreciation**

  Words like "trust" and "commit" call us to recognize our dependence on God, our need for His guidance even in areas where we tend to want to exert our individuality. Often it is difficult for us to "let go" of our own selfish desires and submit ourselves to Him. While learning to depend on God is sometimes difficult, it is not a matter of loss or regret. Instead, we read words like "enjoy" and "delight" and realize that admitting our needs and shortcomings is part of opening ourselves up to receive the refreshing goodness that God wants us to enjoy.

Option: Safe Pasture and More

This option will add five minutes to the Step 3 section.

Call attention to the "God's Part" section of the "Becoming Alert to God's Presence" page. Point out that these are the benefits promised us as we do our parts. Invite volunteers to share what they see God doing for them personally through each of these benefits. Be prepared to add clarifying insights if needed.

- "Safe pasture"—Obviously, no matter how threatening the circumstances, we enjoy the security of God's protective presence. Even when we suffer, His presence gives us the strength to endure.
- "The desires of your heart"—Only by delighting in the Lord can we ever find true satisfaction in life. All other pursuits, no matter how worthwhile, will ultimately leave us unsatisfied.
- "He will make your righteousness shine like the dawn, the justice of your cause like the noonday sun."—The prophet Isaiah bemoaned the fact that when judged by God's perfect standard, "all our righteous acts are like filthy rags" (Isaiah 64:6). But when we commit our ways to Him, He transforms our imperfections, He turns us from our prejudices and biases so that we mature into people who seek righteousness and justice.

Step 4 Option—Making "Faith-Based" Choices (10-15 Minutes)

Remind the class of Elisha's surprising decision to show kindness to the enemy army. We discovered that Elisha's surprising decision to show kindness to the enemy army is an example of making a decision based on faith, instead of what we tend to consider more "rational" criteria. Elisha made his choice based on his awareness of God's control of the situation, and that was centuries before Jesus startled His listeners by telling them, "Love your enemies and pray for those who persecute you" (Matthew 5:44). We're going to explore several passages that mention making choices to see how the advice they give supports what we've discovered about acting in faith.

Have class members return to their small groups of no more than four to six per group. Assign each group one of the following verses to read and discuss. It is not necessary to assign all the verses.

- Deuteronomy 30:19
- Joshua 24:15
- Proverbs 8:10
- Proverbs 16:16
- John 7:17

Instruct the groups to read their verse and discuss the following question: **What difference does awareness of God's presence make in following the instructions of this verse?**

After three minutes, invite a volunteer from each group to share the group's answer to the question. After each group has shared, invite everyone to turn to John 15:16 as a fitting summary to the issue of choices. Read aloud the verse, then comment: **Lest any of us should feel like boasting about the good choices we have made, we regularly need to be reminded that the first and most important choice was made by God. He chose to reach out to us, to reveal to us a valid source and focus for our faith. Only because He first chose to love us are we able to respond to Him in faith.**

Getting Personal

(10 Minutes)

Introduce this time for personal application with the following comment: Of all the times in our lives when our faith should recognize God's presence, our times of prayer should lead the way. However, there probably isn't anyone who has not had the experience of feeling that prayer was just "going through the motions" and feeling as if no one were listening. A typical response when this happens is to just stop praying. People say things such as, "I didn't feel like I was getting through"

or "I wasn't getting anything out of it" so they give up, at least for a time. A far better response when our faith seems inadequate is to make our unawareness of God's presence the focus of our prayer. What better prayer to pray at such a time than to echo the man who exclaimed to Jesus, "I do believe; help me overcome my unbelief!"

Lead the class in a time of prayer centered on the need for increased responsiveness to God's presence. Give these directions: **Feel free to pray silently or to speak aloud, mentioning just one specific situation in which you sense your need to be more aware of God's presence. After someone prays aloud, the next person who prays should repeat the request of the first person before voicing his or her own desire. There will probably be some intervening times of silent reflection and prayer, and that's good.**

Begin this time of prayer, setting an example for honestly and concisely asking for God's help. When time is up, offer a closing prayer.

Getting Personal Option: I'll Be Looking...

This option will add five minutes to the Getting Personal section.

Conclude this session by having class members return to their earlier small groups. Instruct group members—starting with the person whose driver's license expires soonest—to share situations in which they intend to be consciously looking for God's presence in the coming week. **Just as it's possible to miss a beautiful sunset by keeping our eyes focused on the ground ahead of us, it is probably very common for people to miss sensing God's presence because of preoccupation with life's details. One way to break out of that pattern is to train our hearts and minds to be on the lookout for evidences of God.**

Share one thing you intend to do, then invite others to share similarly.

Before participants leave announce: **The next session will focus on obedience as an expression of our faith. We'll take a look at an exciting incident from Scripture which powerfully illustrates the vital link between obedience and faith.**

I Notice God When...

List on this sheet any circumstances which tend to make you aware of God.

Places

Times

People

I Notice God When...

Situations

Other

Becoming Alert to God's Presence

Our Part	God's Part
"**Trust** in the Lord and **do good**; **dwell** in the land and **enjoy**	safe pasture."
"**Delight** yourself in the Lord	and he will give you the desires of your heart."
"**Commit** your way to the Lord; **trust** in him	and he will do this: He will make your righteousness shine like the dawn, the justice of your cause like the noonday sun" (Psalm 37:3-6).

Notice the words in boldface type. They call us to specific actions and attitudes which will bring great benefits. Beside each phrase repeated below, describe at least two specific ways you can put that action or attitude into practice in your life.

Trust in the Lord

Becoming Alert to God's Presence

Do good

Dwell in the land

Enjoy safe pasture

Delight yourself in the Lord

Commit your way to the Lord

Trust in him

Learning to Trust God © 1997 by Gospel Light. Permission to photocopy granted.

Faith: Acting in Obedience

Session Keys

Key Verses

"Shadrach, Meshach and Abednego replied to the king, 'O Nebuchadnezzar, we do not need to defend ourselves before you in this matter. If we are thrown into the blazing furnace, the God we serve is able to save us from it, and he will rescue us from your hand, O king. But even if he does not, we want you to know, O king, that we will not serve your gods or worship the image of gold you have set up.'" Daniel 3:16-18

Key Idea

Faith requires that we are obedient to God in all situations, even when facing great personal risks.

Biblical Basis

Exodus 4:13,15; Deuteronomy 4:9; 31:6; Joshua 1:6,7; Judges 4:8; 6:15; 1 Kings 19:3; 1 Chronicles 22:13; 2 Chronicles 19:11; Jeremiah 1:6; Ezekiel 16:49; Daniel 3; Jonah 1:3; Micah 6:8; Matthew 14:27; 28:19,20; Luke 6:27,28; 11:28; Acts 23:11; 27:22,25; Romans 14:19; 1 Corinthians 16:13,14; 2 Corinthians 12:7-10; Galatians 5:14; Ephesians 4:32; Philippians 1:20; Colossians 3:16; Hebrews 11:32-39; James 1:27; 1 Peter 2:18-23; 5:6-10

Background

Three boys stood tall while music played
They would not bow, they weren't afraid.
Threats and anger would not make
Them disobey—God's law forsake.

Three boys stood in that burning fire.
While scorching flames kept leaping higher
Those flames reached up to Shadrach's chin,
But couldn't scorch their hair or skin.

The reasons we sometimes give for not serving God sound pathetically inadequate compared to the excuse Shadrach, Meshach, and Abednego could have given. For example, a few typical excuses heard in today's churches:

"I really can't _____(insert opportunity to serve)_____ because I really need that time for myself."

"I shouldn't be expected to _____(another possibility to help)____ because I've done my turn."

"I'm sure there must be someone who could do it better."

"I'm just too busy at work and with my family, and soccer, and...you know how it is."

If anyone ever had a valid reason for backing away from serving God, it was Shadrach, Meshach and Abednego. Agreeing to serve was not just inconvenient for them, it was life threatening!

Why aren't we more like those young men? Perhaps it is because we have not discovered the joy of serving God "with all our hearts." There is no hint in Daniel 3 that Shadrach, Meshach and Abednego were serving God out of a sense of duty. They were not just going along with what they thought was expected of them. Instead, they were powerfully motivated by their faith. Because they saw their lives through the eyes of faith, seeing their situation from God's perspective, they wanted to serve Him, regardless of the consequences.

Think about your reason for serving by teaching adults. Are you allowing your faith to show you that God is helping you to make a difference in someone's life? Stepping out and serving God, doing what you know is right—even before you see results, even when risks and problems get in the way—is a demonstration of the same faith that carried those three young men through an ordeal far more harrowing than any group of adult learners.

Preparation

- Provide blank name tags and felt-tip pens. Make a tag for yourself.
- On a table at the front of the room, provide materials for one of the following Getting Started choices:
    - **Choice 1: What If...?**—On a blank transparency or on the chalkboard, write the following incomplete question:
    "What if I _____ (action in obedience to God) __ and it doesn't work?"
    Provide three or four places for writing: on the chalkboard, additional transparencies, and/or large sheets of newsprint or butcher paper. Have available chalk, transparency markers, and/or felt-tip pens for group members to use.
    - **Choice 2: Signs of Seeds Sprouting!**—Reproduce copies of the "Signs of Seeds Sprouting!" handout on page 53, providing one copy per person. Provide pens or pencils for those who need them.
- Reproduce copies of the "Shadrach, Meshach and Abednego" handout on pages 51-52 and the "Gaining the Courage to Obey" handout on pages 54-53, providing one copy per person.
- Provide several "sticky notes" for each person.
- Start Option: Reluctant Heroes—Six sheets of colored paper, with one of the following names and references written on them: Moses (Exodus 4:13); Barak (Judges 4:8); Gideon (Judges 6:15); Elijah (1 Kings 19:3); Jeremiah (Jeremiah 1:6); Jonah (Jonah 1:3).
- Step 4 Option: Some Calls to Action—Provide blank writing paper and pens or pencils for each participant.
- Provide Bibles for participants who may not have them.

Session 3 at a Glance

SECTION	ONE-SESSION PLAN		TWO-SESSION PLAN	WHAT YOU'LL DO
Time Schedule	60 to 75 Minutes	More than 75 Minutes	60 Minutes (each session)	
Getting Started	10	10-20	20	Get Acquainted—Introduce obedience and faith
Getting into the Word	40	60-75	40	
Step 1 Shadrach, Meshach and Abednego Serve God	10	20	20	Examine the active faith of the three Hebrews
Step 2 Is It Worth the Risk?	15	20	20	Evaluate the pros and cons of full obedience
			Session 2 Start Option: 10	
Step 3 Gaining the Courage to Obey	15	20	20	Discuss ways to dispel fears and build courage
(Step 4 Option) Some Calls to Action	(10)	(10)	15	Investigate selected commands in Scripture
Getting Personal	10	10-15	15	Putting faith into action

Session Plan

Leader's Choice

Two-Meeting Track: This session is designed to be completed in one 60- to 75-minute meeting. If you want to extend the session over two meetings and allow group members more time for discussion, **END** your first meeting and **BEGIN** your second meeting at the stop-and-go symbol in the session plan.

The boxes marked with the clock symbol provide optional learning experiences to extend this session over two meetings or to accommodate a session longer than 60 to 75 minutes.

Getting Started

(10 Minutes)

Choice 1—What If...?

Welcome group members as they arrive and suggest they make and wear name tags.

Call their attention to the partial statement you wrote on a transparency or on the chalkboard: **What if I _____(action in obedience to God)_____ and it doesn't work?** Give the following instruction: **Think of at least one action you have felt at some point in your life that God wanted you to do, but you were fearful to try it. Then go to the chalkboard (or blank transparencies or sheets of paper) and write a phrase to complete the "What if...?" statement.** As others arrive, encourage them to join in.

After several minutes, ask group members to be seated, then ask for a show of hands of those who felt at least a twinge of guilt in recalling an example of being fearful to obey God. (Probably most hands will go up.) Then invite volunteers to read aloud the phrases group members wrote.

Conclude this Getting Started activity by introducing the topic for this session: **If God only called us to do things we felt confident in doing or were already inclined to do, we'd have little or no need for faith. Today we're going to look at the challenge of responding in faith when something we know we should do feels threatening, as though we would be "in over our heads."**

Choice 2—Signs of Seeds Sprouting!

Welcome group members as they arrive and suggest they make and wear name tags.

Distribute copies of the "Signs of Seeds Sprouting!" handout, providing pens or pencils to those who need them. Encourage members to work individually for a few minutes, recounting any evidence of new growth in their faith.

After several minutes, ask for a show of hands of those who were able to write that their faith has grown immensely and they've been able to overcome all doubts and hesitancies. (Probably no one will respond.) Next, ask how many wrote something to indicate that their faith is still a long way from perfection. (Probably most hands will go up.) Then ask how many were able to write about some evidences that their faith has grown.

Invite volunteers from the last group who raised their hands to read aloud all or part of what they wrote about growing in faith. Then comment: **One of the best ways to help your faith grow is to periodically reflect on ways it has grown in the past. When you recall a time when God responded, when you were aware of His presence, your faith is encouraged. And when you share those experiences, our** faith is encouraged, also. Today we're going to explore another way our faith grows—by acting in obedience to God, even in the face of inward doubts or outward pressures.

Getting Started Option: I Think I Can! I Think I Can!

This option will add 10 minutes to the Getting Started section.

After completing one of the Getting Started activities, say: **Many people equate faith with the famous children's story of the little engine that huffed and puffed its way up the hill by saying over and over, "I think I can! I think I can!"** As we will continue to see in this series, true faith is much more than wishful or even positive thinking. Still, there is always value in looking beyond the problem to envision the solution, or in looking back on previous "mountains" and recalling our experiences in getting to the top.

Instruct class members to form groups of two or three and share with each other an incident from their experience when they faced what seemed to be an insurmountable problem, but in which they ultimately succeeded. Their incidents need not be directly related to faith in God, but simply examples of achieving something that seemed difficult if not impossible.

After a few minutes of interaction, invite volunteers to tell the group about an incident they heard someone else tell them. Then lead into today's study with this comment: **All of us can identify with the positive feelings which come from finally winning out over a major obstacle. We can also empathize with the earlier feelings of doubt, frustration or fear. But, it's doubtful that any of us have ever had to face a challenge as threatening as the one we are going to examine in today's study.**

Getting into the Word

(40 Minutes)

Step 1—Shadrach, Meshach and Abednego Serve God (10 Minutes)

Ask the class: **What do you remember about the famous Bible story of Shadrach, Meshach and Abednego?** As class members mention things they recall, list them on the chalkboard or a blank overhead transparency. Overlook any errors in what they say. After all, you did ask them to tell what they remembered. If someone shares an obviously incomplete fact, ask questions to jog the group's memory. For example, if someone says, "I think Shadrach, Meshach and Abednego were captives, but I don't remember where," ask the class: **Does anyone remember the ancient empire which held these young men captive?**

Once the major outline of the story has been shared, distribute the "Shadrach, Meshach and Abednego" handout. Divide the class into thirds, and within each third form smaller groups of no more than five or six per group. Assign those in each third one section from the handout:

The Challenge (Daniel 3:1-12)
The Confrontation (Daniel 3:12-23)
The Conclusion (Daniel 3:24-30)

Instruct the groups to read their part of the story and then work together to answer the questions in their section of the handout. Allow three to four minutes for groups to work, then invite volunteers to share their answers to the questions.

Notice that the questions require that group members think about what they read, not just find information to fill in the blanks. While such questions do stimulate interest, they can result in a range of responses, and class members may get sidetracked. Therefore, encourage creative thought, but be sure to bring the discussion to a conclusion by calling attention to Nebuchadnezzar's insight into the basis for the courageous stand by Shadrach and his friends: "They trusted in him" (v. 28).

After the discussion say: **The rest of this session will explore the kind of trust which made three young men willing to give up their lives rather than serve or worship any god except their own God.**

Option: A Crowd of Heroes

This option will add 10 minutes to the Step 1 section.

Point out that Shadrach, Meshach and Abednego are mentioned in passing in the list of heroes in Hebrews 11. Verse 34 refers to them (without giving their names), as having "quenched the fury of the flames." Read aloud Hebrews 11:32-35—a stirring list of people who triumphed through faith. Then ask a volunteer to read aloud Hebrews 11:35-38, which honors others who also had faith, but who suffered and died. Ask: **What is different about the people I read about and those that (class member) read about?** Even though the latter group did not experience a miraculous rescue, what evidence is in these verses that the lack of deliverance was not due to lack of faith on their part? (Verse 38 says, "the world was not worthy of them," and verse 39 begins, "These were all commended for their faith.")

What do these two groups of heroes and the two declarations of Shadrach and his friends (see Daniel 3:17,18) **say to you about faith?** Make sure the point is clearly made that faith is not a magic formula designed to guarantee our desires. Instead, faith is acting in obedient trust that God is truly in control, regardless of the initial outcome. This concept will be explored more fully in Step 2.

Note: The phrase "But even if he does not" (v. 18) may be taken by some as an exaggerated expression of the unthinkable along the lines of "even if the sky should fall!" However, it is best to accept statements at face value unless there is strong evidence indicating otherwise. In this case, the most likely understanding of the phrase is that Shadrach and his friends had committed themselves to obeying God even if they lost their lives by so doing.

Step 2—Is It Worth the Risk? (15 Minutes)

Comment: King Nebuchadnezzar declared his admiration for the courageous faith of Shadrach and his friends. And knowing how the story ended, we can echo his conviction. However, when it comes to putting faith into action in our own lives, we often struggle with the question, What if God doesn't come through for me? Will I be like Peter stepping out of the boat and then floundering because of the storm and my imperfect faith? Fortunately, the Bible does not look at life through rose-colored glasses. It is very firmly rooted in the realities of life's struggles. We're going to look at three New Testament passages to help us better understand the true meaning of living by faith in a fallen world.

With class members in the same small groups as earlier, assign one of the following passages to each group:
- 2 Corinthians 12:7-10
- 1 Peter 2:18-23
- 1 Peter 5:6-10

Instruct the groups to read their passages, then discuss the following questions (write these on the board or an overhead transparency):

1. What do these verses say about why God sometimes allows us to endure hardships, even when we are trusting in Him?
2. How can these verses help when we are fearful about doing what is right?
3. How can we deal with the fear that maybe God won't do what we are hoping?
4. Which verse in this passage is most encouraging to your faith?

Give the groups four to six minutes to discuss, then invite volunteers from each group to share their answers to the questions. Then ask: What are the pluses which come from acting on our faith in God? What are the potential minuses that tend to keep us from putting our faith into action?

Accept responses, being sensitive to comments which indicate a person may be struggling to put faith into action. Encourage participants to keep their hearts and minds open to learn more of what Scripture teaches about faith.

Option: An Encouraging Word

This option will add five minutes to the Step 2 section.

Distribute sticky notes to everyone, along with pens or pencils for those who need them. Give the following instructions: In your groups, agree on one verse from the passage you just explored that you find encouraging to your faith. Go around the group, assigning each person a word from the verse to write on a sticky note. Continue until all words have been assigned and written. Then collect all your sticky notes in random order and exchange them with another group. Then, work together to put your new verse in correct order.

After two minutes, invite volunteers to read aloud the verse they arranged. Ask: Why do you think another group selected this verse as being encouraging to their faith?

Note: If you are completing this session in one meeting, ignore this break and continue with Step 3.

Two-Meeting Track: If you want to spread this session over two meetings, **STOP** here and close in prayer. Inform group members that your next meeting will focus on gaining the courage to obey what we believe God wants us to do.

Start Option: Reluctant Heroes (10 Minutes)

Welcome group members as they arrive and suggest they make and wear name tags.

Before everyone arrives, list the following names and references on six colored sheets of paper: Moses (Exodus 4:13); Barak (Judges 4:8); Gideon (Judges 6:15); Elijah (1 Kings 19:3); Jeremiah (Jeremiah 1:6); Jonah (Jonah 1:3). Mount the papers in prominent places on the walls. Across the top of the chalkboard or on an overhead transparency, write "I felt like _____ when _____."

As members arrive, welcome them and talk informally about their week's activities. Then call attention to the names you have displayed. Ask everyone to choose one name and look up the reference to see how that hero felt when God called him to do an important job.

Allow a minute or so for group members to locate and read their verse. Ask for volunteers to tell how their character felt when God called them. Then ask for a show of hands of those who have ever felt like one of those characters. Invite volunteers to tell of a time when they felt like Moses or Gideon or one of the other "heroes" when faced with something you believed God wanted you to do. Be prepared to share a similar incident from your own experience.

Step 3—Gaining the Courage to Obey (15 Minutes)

Distribute copies of the "Gaining the Courage to Obey" handout, pointing out the question below the nine verses. Ask for a volunteer whose middle name begins with the letters A, B or C to read aloud the first verse on the page. Continue similarly with the remaining verses. If no one in your class has a middle name starting with the letters in front of a verse, ask for anyone with a first name, then a last name starting with one of those letters.

After all nine verses have been read aloud, invite volunteers to share the insights these verses gave them about gaining the courage to do the right thing. Be prepared to add one or more of the following comments to stimulate thought or to clarify ideas presented by class members:

• The frequent repetition of the call to be courageous clearly indicates that the lack of courage is a common problem. If all of God's people were automatically filled with the courage and the desire to do right, there would have been no need for so many exhortations. Knowing that others share this problem does not by itself produce courage, but it does reduce the pressure of feeling uniquely incompetent or unworthy.

- Courage to do what is right is either clearly stated or obviously implied to be linked to a relationship with God. He is the ultimate source of the qualities we need in order to fulfill what He asks us to do. In other words, He never asks us to do something for which He does not provide the wherewithal to do it.
- Courage is always linked with actions much more than with feelings. The question is never, Do you feel brave? Instead, the challenge is, Will you act in faith in spite of your doubts and fears?
- Many of these exhortations were spoken directly by God, an angel or Jesus. Others were the words of ordinary mortals. It is easy to claim that if God would send an angel, we would eagerly respond. However, Scripture seems to indicate that those who were visited by God had as much trouble acting in faith as anyone else. Remember Moses and the burning bush? God provided dramatic evidence of who He was and how He would go with Moses, yet Moses still asked God to find someone else for the job (see Exodus 4:15).
- Courageous obedience involves a decision. Each challenge to take courage clearly sets in front of us a choice of how to act in a difficult situation. Courage is not imposed upon us from the outside, although God is the ultimate source. Courage is the act of stepping out, taking the plunge to do the very best we know, while trusting God for the result.

Option: Exercising Your Faith

This option will add five minutes to the Step 3 section.

Comment: Often the reason we do not take the initiative to put our faith into action is not so much because of fear, but simply because we don't want to do something. Our lack of faithful obedience sometimes comes down to an unwillingness to exert ourselves or a reluctance to do something we feel is unpleasant. We resist doing something just because we feel we ought to.

Ask: What are some words of advice we can give to each other that would encourage us to do the right thing in spite of feelings that pull us away from obedience? Be prepared to share a suggestion or two that you have found helpful. A few approaches you might mention are:

- Make up your mind—in advance—that you want to be a person who puts faith into action. Rather than waiting to make up your mind when presented with an opportunity, commit yourself to becoming an obedient servant now.
- Pray before deciding. Rather than asking God to give you some indication if you *should* accept an opportunity to serve, ask Him to indicate if you should *not* get involved.
- Ask yourself, If I don't do this, what will I be doing instead? Which is more likely to produce positive results in my life and the lives of others?

Step 4 Option: Some Calls to Action (10-15 Minutes)

Give each group member a sheet of paper and a pen or pencil as needed. Read aloud

the words of Jesus from Luke 11:28: "'Blessed rather are those who hear the word of God and obey it.'" Ask group members to write down the following references as you write them on the chalkboard or an overhead transparency.

- Deuteronomy 4:9
- Ezekiel 16:49
- Micah 6:8
- Matthew 28:19,20
- Luke 6:27,28
- Romans 14:19
- Galatians 5:14
- Ephesians 4:32
- Colossians 3:16
- James 1:27

Comment: **Lest any of you says you would love to put your faith into action if you just knew what it was God wanted you to do, these ten references are clear statements of important actions to which God calls us.**

Instruct everyone to choose one of the verses and take a full two minutes to write on their papers specific ways in which they could be showing their faith by obeying that command.

When the minute is up, point to the first reference and ask for a show of hands of those who read it. Count the hands and write the number next to that reference. Continue similarly for all ten. Then invite volunteers who read whichever verse was chosen by the most group members to read aloud the verse and share the actions they thought of. List these actions on the chalkboard or an overhead transparency.

Encourage group members to add to their lists any actions mentioned which they feel they could be doing. Continue similarly for as many other references as time allows. Conclude this segment by again reading aloud Jesus' words from Luke 11:28.

Getting Personal

(10 Minutes)

Have group members return to the same small groups they were in earlier. Starting with the person in each group who most recently read the Bible at home, everyone shares one action from their lists (from Step 4 Option) that they feel they need to start doing or to do more often and why they chose that action. After each person has shared, have group members pray for each other, asking God's help to follow through in putting faith into action in practical ways.

Note: If the class did not do the Step 4 Option, ask the small group members to spend a few minutes reading the verses listed in Step 4 together. As the verses are read, ask each person to choose a verse that particularly speaks to him or her. Give everyone a minute or two to decide on an action that is suggested, then have them share with their small group members what that action should be. After each person has shared, have group members pray for each other, asking God's help to follow through in putting faith into action in practical ways.

Getting Personal Option: What I Plan to Do

This option will add five minutes to the Getting Personal section.

As groups finish praying together, instruct them to make one more round of their small groups, this time with everyone identifying at least one specific situation in which they intend to implement their selected action. Encourage them to be as precise as possible, avoiding vague generalities. Be prepared to share an example of your own as a model.

Before participants leave announce: **The next session will focus on how our faith impacts our relationships with others, even people we don't like.**

Shadrach, Meshach and Abednego

The Challenge (Daniel 3:1-12)

1. What pressures did Shadrach and his friends face in this passage?

2. What seems to have been the attitude of the Babylonians towards Shadrach and his friends? Why?

3. What possible options did Shadrach and his friends have?

4. What reasons could Shadrach and his friends have used to justify obeying the king's command?

The Confrontation (Daniel 3:12-23)

1. Why do you think Nebuchadnezzar was so angry? In light of that, why do you think he gave Shadrach and his friends a second chance to obey his decree?

2. Put yourself in Shadrach's place. Do you imagine it was harder or easier to stand up to the king face-to-face than to have originally refused to worship his image? Why?

3. Look again at verses 17 and 18. Compare the level of faith demonstrated by these two statements: "The God we serve...**will rescue us** from your hand....**But even if he does not**,...we will not serve your gods...."

The Conclusion (Daniel 3:24-30)

1. Besides surviving the furnace, what resulted from the faithful obedience of Shadrach and his friends?

2. What do you suppose one of the Babylonian officials might have said as he examined Shadrach and his friends?

3. What did Nebuchadnezzar cite as the reason Shadrach and his friends resisted his decree?

Signs of Seeds Sprouting!

Mark the responses which are closest to what you would say. Then on the comment lines, write what you really would say.

1. Evidences I've seen of new growth in my faith:

_____ Nothing.
_____ My prayers seem more purposeful.
_____ The Bible seems to speak more directly to me.
_____ Meeting with other believers is more important to me than before.
_____ Church is more fun.
_____ I'm more aware of ways in which I can serve God and others.

Comment:

_____

_____

_____

Signs of Seeds Sprouting!

2. Recently, I feel that my faith has grown:

_____ Not at all. I've got more doubts than ever.
_____ Perhaps a little bit. I'm not sure, but I'm hopeful.
_____ Enough to notice, but I'm still a long way from perfection.
_____ Significantly, giving me increasing confidence and trust.
_____ Immensely! I've been able to overcome doubts and hesitancies.

Comment:

_____

_____

_____

Gaining the Courage to Obey

Read the following verses:

A/B/C—"Be strong and courageous. Do not be afraid or terrified because of them, for the LORD your God goes with you, he will never leave you nor forsake you" (Deuteronomy 31:6).

D/E/F—"Be strong and courageous....Be strong and very courageous" (Joshua 1:6,7).

G/H/I—"Then you will have success if you are careful to observe the decrees and laws that the LORD gave Moses for Israel. Be strong and courageous. Do not be afraid or discouraged" (1 Chronicles 22:13).

J/K/L—"Act with courage, and may the LORD be with those who do well" (2 Chronicles 19:11).

M/N/O—"'Take courage! It is I [Jesus]. Don't be afraid'" (Matthew 14:27).

P/Q/R—"Take courage!" (Acts 23:11).

S/T— "'But now I urge you to keep up your courage....So keep up your courage, men, for I have faith in God'" (Acts 27:22,25).

U/V/W—"Be on your guard; stand firm in the faith; be men of courage; be strong. Do everything in love" (1 Corinthians 16:13,14).

X/Y/Z —"I eagerly expect and hope that I will in no way be ashamed, but will have sufficient courage so that now as always Christ will be **exalted** in my body, whether by life or by death" (Philippians 1:20).

What insights do these verses give about gaining the courage to do the right things we know we should?

1.

2

3.

4.

5

Faith: Accepting and Loving Others

Session Keys

Key Verses

"For in Christ neither circumcision nor uncircumcision has any value. The only thing that counts is faith expressing itself through love." Galatians 5:6

"And we know that in all things God works for the good of those who love him, who have been called according to his purpose." Romans 8:28

Key Idea

Knowing that God loves and accepts all people, faith is required to love and accept even those we find hard to like.

Biblical Basis

Leviticus 19:18; Deuteronomy 7:7,8; 10:17-21; Jeremiah 48:42,47; Ezekiel 18:21-23; Jonah 1—4; John 4:7-9; 13:34; 14:21; Acts 10:28; Romans 5:8; 8:28; 15:1,2; 1 Corinthians 12:13; 2 Corinthians 5:14,15; Galatians 5:6; Ephesians 2:4,5,11-13; Colossians 3:12-14; 1 Peter 3:9

Background

Jonah had a great big fish,
   great big fish,
   great big fish.
Jonah had a great big fish,
   Or really, it had Jonah.

Jonah had a great big grudge,
   great big grudge,
   great big grudge.
Jonah had a great big grudge,
   But God had other plans.

The young soccer player was being carried off the far side of the field. It was obvious his injury was not trivial. One of the parents on the near side was heard to mutter, "Well, he got what he deserved. He's been asking for it the whole game."

Human nature tends to relish seeing someone get their "comeuppance," especially if we feel that person had previously offended us. Jonah is the prime example in Scripture of this common desire for revenge. While Jonah had ample belief in God's power and goodness, he had not allowed his faith to transform his own attitude. He did not want God to show mercy. Jonah had allowed his status as one of God's chosen people to color his view of all other people. Jonah wanted to confine God's love to the limits of Jonah's standards, rather than allowing his attitude toward others to be expanded to the size of God's love.

Sharing love when we don't feel loving is an act of faith. Loving our enemies is a demonstration of trust that God's love will change things. Sometimes it is the other person who is changed by our faithful loving. And sometimes it is our own attitude that God must alter.

Is there a member of your class who is hard for you to love? Is there a person in your life you find it uncomfortable to reach out to? Do you struggle with getting to know unchurched neighbors? Are you frustrated by coworkers who are more work than help? Are you reluctant to take the initiative to assist someone you know is in need? Faith enables us to move beyond our circle of comfort, loving those we once disliked—even those we are still not fond of!

Preparation

- Provide blank name tags and felt-tips pens. Make a tag for yourself.
- On a table at the front of the room, provide materials for one of these Getting Started choices:
  - **Choice 1: People Who Bug Me**—Provide a large sheet of newsprint and several felt-tip pens for each group of from four to six members. Also have a roll of masking tape available. On an extra sheet of paper write the following heading in large letters: "People Who Bug Me." Mount the paper on a wall in the room.
  - **Choice 2: If I Were the Judge**—Reproduce copies of the "If I Were the Judge" handout on page 69, providing one copy per person. Provide pens or pencils for those who need them.
- Option: There Goes the Neighborhood—A chalkboard and chalk, or an overhead projector, blank transparency and transparency pen. Divide the board or the transparency into four sections. In each section, write one of the following references: Jeremiah 48:42,47; John 4:7-9; Acts 10:28; 1 Corinthians 12:13.
- Reproduce copies of the "Love As an Act of Faith" handout on pages 70-71, providing one copy per person.
- Provide a large sheet of newsprint and two or three felt-tip pens for every four to six class members.
- Provide blank paper and pens or pencils for each participant.
- Provide Bibles for those who do not bring one.

- Step 4 Option: On five large sheets of newsprint or butcher paper, use a broad-tipped felt pen to write the words of Deuteronomy 10:17-21—one verse on each sheet. On each sheet, omit some of the key words, drawing blanks in their places. For example:

"For the Lord your God is _____ and

_____ , the _____ God,

_____ and _____ , who shows no

_____ and accepts no _____ ."

Continue similarly with all five verses. Then roll up the sheets and secure them with rubber bands until time to use them in Step 4 Option.

Session 4 at a Glance

SECTION	ONE-SESSION PLAN		TWO-SESSION PLAN	WHAT YOU'LL DO
Time Schedule	60 to 75 Minutes	More than 75 Minutes	60 Minutes (each session)	
Getting Started	10	10-20	20	Get Acquainted—Introduce topic of relationships and faith
Getting into the Word	40	60-75	40	
Step 1 Jonah's Prejudice Meets God's Mercy	10	20	20	Contrast Jonah's attitude with God's attitude
Step 2 Love As an Act of Faith	15	20	20	Examine Scriptures which portray love as action
			Session 2 Start Option: 10	
Step 3 Learning to Love Those We Don't Even Like	15	20	20	Discuss ways to show love when we don't feel loving
(Step 4 Option) Limits We Try to Impose on God	(10)	(15)	15	Identify ways we try to squeeze God to fit our narrow views
Getting Personal	10	10-15	15	Spend time in prayer

Session Plan

Leader's Choice

Two-Meeting Track: This session is designed to be completed in one 60- to 75-minute meeting. If you want to extend the session over two meetings and allow group members more time for discussion, **END** your first meeting and **BEGIN** your second meeting at the stop-and-go symbol in the session plan.

The boxes marked with the clock symbol provide optional learning experiences to extend this session over two meetings or to accommodate a session longer than 60 to 75 minutes.

Getting Started

(10 Minutes)

Choice 1—People Who Bug Me

Welcome group members as they arrive and suggest they make and wear name tags.

Ask participants to form groups of no more than six members. Using felt-tip pens and large sheets of paper, have them work together to list and illustrate characteristics of people whom they find annoying or difficult.

As groups finish their illustrated lists, have them tape them on the walls around the room. Ask volunteers to read aloud the descriptions they wrote. Then ask: **Why do we tend to find people like this so unpleasant and hard to like?** After several group members respond, lead into the rest of the session with this comment: **One of the great problems which has always plagued the human race is that many of us cause many others to dislike us. And we dislike them back. Today we're going to explore how faith impacts our relationships, especially our relationships with those people who are hard for us to like.**

Choice 2—If I Were the Judge

Welcome group members as they arrive and suggest they make and wear name tags.

Give each person a copy of the "If I Were the Judge" handout and a pen or pencil. Encourage them to work with no more than three or four other group members to compile a list of "Annoying Offenses" and "Appropriate Penalties."

After several minutes in which group members talk and write, share two or three offenses and penalties from your paper. Then invite volunteers to each read one or two from their handouts. After all groups have shared, introduce this session's topic by commenting: **There seems to be almost no limit to the ways in which human beings can offend each other. And each offense further strains whatever bonds link us together, often causing us to view others as problems or even as enemies, rather than as fellow humans created by God. Today we are going to explore the impact of faith on our relationships, especially with those people who are hard for us to like.**

Getting Started Option: There Goes the Neighborhood

This option will add 10 minutes to the Getting Started section.

After completing one of the Getting Started activities, comment: **The Bible contains many stories about people who were viewed as inferior or unworthy. Usually these judgments were justified, for those people truly deserved the harshest criticism.** Let's look at some statements in the Bible about some of these difficult kinds

of people. Divide the room into fourths. Assign one of the four Scripture passages you already listed on the chalkboard or transparency to the group members in each quarter of the room.

Instruct group members to find and read their assigned passages, looking for evidence of God's dealings with different groups of people.

After two or three minutes, invite a volunteer from each section to read the assigned passage aloud, and have him or her tell what was discovered about God's attitude toward people who at one time were in opposition to Him. After this sharing, ask half of the class to turn to Ephesians 2:11-13 where Paul addressed Gentile Christians. Ask the rest of the class to find Ezekiel 18:21-23. Ask for a volunteer to read the verses aloud. Then comment: **Had Jonah been in the church at Ephesus, it is likely that he would have found it very hard to swallow Paul's words to the Gentiles. He probably would not have enjoyed Ezekiel's message either. Jonah is typical of so many people who want to claim God's mercies for themselves, but wish for God's wrath on their enemies.**

Getting into the Word

(40 Minutes)

Step 1—Jonah's Prejudice Meets God's Mercy (10 Minutes)

Ask: **What's the first thought that pops into your head when I say the name "Jonah"?** Most group members are likely to answer: "and the whale" or "and the big fish." Some might suggest "trying to run away from God." It is unlikely that many will say their first thought is "prejudice." Point this out to the class, then comment: **While the fish gets all the attention, a great many people totally miss one of the major points of this famous story: Jonah is the classic example in Scripture of racial, social and religious prejudice. Jonah did not want to preach in Nineveh, not because he feared the Assyrians, but because he did not want them to have the chance to repent. Jonah knew that if they repented, God would show mercy and withhold the judgment Jonah deeply wanted to see imposed upon that great but wicked city** (see Jonah 4:1,2).

Ask for three volunteers who like to read. Assign each volunteer one of the following parts to read: Jonah, God, or narrator. Instruct them to read Jonah 3:10—4:11 aloud, each one reading his or her assigned part. Point out to the class that this concluding section of the book comes after the incident with the storm and the fish. When Jonah agreed to obey God, he went to Nineveh and delivered the warning God had entrusted to him. The Ninevites, including their king, believed God, went into mourning and earnestly prayed that God would spare them.

After the reading, discuss the following questions:

Why do you think it was so hard for Jonah to give up his prejudice and anger? How similar is that to our own intolerances of other people?

According to these verses, what was the basis for God's decision to spare the city?

Reread Jonah's description of God in Jonah 4:2. It is obvious that Jonah did not intend this description as a compliment. What kind of a God do you think Jonah would have preferred? What happens when we try to squeeze God to fit into our preconceived notions?

Read Jonah 4:2 one more time. How common today is Jonah's dislike of God's compassion being extended to all people?

Think of some people whose behavior offends or upsets you to the point you almost wish God were not as Jonah described him.

After the discussion, ask for a show of hands of those who can understand Jonah's desire to exclude the Assyrians from receiving God's mercy. Summarize this segment of the session: Obviously, we all have areas or degrees of intolerance and prejudice. Let's continue in this session to see how our faith impacts those very human—and very sinful—attitudes.

Option: A Very Abrupt Ending

This option will add 10 minutes to the Step 1 section.

Ask a group member to again read aloud Jonah 4:10,11. Ask: **Why do you think the book ends with God's question to Jonah?** Several reasons seem reasonable. From a stylistic viewpoint, this gives God both the last word and the first word in this book, emphasizing His loving forgiveness. Also, the answer to the question is obvious. No reply is really needed. Besides, not knowing Jonah's reply pushes the reader to keep wrestling with the issue raised in the book, feeling a need to frame a personal response to God's question. Will we align ourselves with the sulking, bigoted Jonah? Or will we agree with God's concern for the needs of all people of the world?

Give everyone a piece of paper and a pen or pencil if needed. Have members write a response that Jonah might have made to the question God asked. Encourage them to imagine how Jonah would have responded. Did he continue to resent God's concern for Nineveh? Did he grudgingly submit to God's benevolence? Did he repent of his narrow-mindedness and actively embrace the Assyrian brothers and sisters who were created, loved and redeemed by the same God who created, loved and redeemed the people of Israel? Allow two or three minutes for group members to write, then invite volunteers to read their answers aloud.

Step 2—Love As an Act of Faith (15 Minutes)

Comment: The story of Jonah clearly teaches that God's love extends to all people, not just a select few. Also, by enlisting Jonah to be the agent by which that love was communicated, the story calls God's people to actively reach out to those who are estranged from God. The challenge for most of us is, how can we show love to people we don't like?

Write the following phrases on the chalkboard or overhead transparency: "Falling in Love" and "Love at First Sight." Ask: **What idea about love do these familiar phrases convey?** Accept responses from the class. Be ready to clarify their comments with the following ideas: **These phrases reflect a view that love—romantic love—is an involuntary response to something or someone. It just happens to us. A person is either "in love" or not.**

After group members respond, share this comment: **These popular views of love permeate our society. Because of that, they color our understanding of God's love, even though they have nothing to do with either the love God bestows on us or the love He calls us to exhibit to others. The concept of romantic or sexual love was conveyed in Greek by a word (*eros*) which is not even used in the New Testament. The two Greek words which the New Testament does use reflect two distinct kinds of love: *phileo* (tender affection) and *agapao* (acting in the best interest of the other person). While *phileo* will produce beneficial actions (i.e. the noun *philanthropia* is translated "kindness" in Acts 28:2 and Titus 3:4), such actions are seen to grow out of loving feelings. On the other hand, *agapao* may involve feelings, but the emphasis is on actions which are intentionally chosen. God's love and Christian *agape* love as its outgrowth is not an impulsive response to warm feelings; it is an action seeking to benefit the other person.**

Distribute copies of the "Love As an Act of Faith" handout. Ask everyone to silently read the "One way of saying it" statement at the top of sheet. Ask: **What do you see as the difference between the two types of love described in this statement? What would be an example of the first kind of love** (an emotional response to someone perceived as being lovable)? **What would be an example of the second kind of love** (a pattern of actions intended to help someone become lovable)?

Ask each person to choose one of the Scriptures listed on the handout and look for how the love described there is a demonstration of faith. After a minute or two, invite volunteers to read aloud the verse(s) they chose and tell what evidence of faith they found there. (In each case, and repeatedly throughout Scripture, love is seen as a powerful force which makes a difference in people's lives. To act in love towards someone, not because that person deserves it, but simply in order to bring benefit to that person, is an act of belief that change for the better is possible in that person's life.)

After several group members respond, ask everyone to write a completion to the statement at the bottom of the handout page: **Seeking God's best for a person I don't like is demonstrating my faith that....** Allow a minute or two, then invite volunteers to read their statements aloud.

Option: Prayer For God's Help

This option will add five minutes to the Step 2 section.

Let's take some time to pray for God's help in actively loving a person who we don't find lovable. Ask everyone to think of a specific person or group of persons for whom they find it hard to have feelings of tender affection. Invite volunteers to offer one-sentence prayers, confessing negative feelings towards those people, and asking for help in showing love to them. Instruct group members not to mention anyone by name in these prayers.

Note: If you are completing this session in one meeting, ignore this break and continue with Step 3.

Two-Meeting Track: If you want to spread this session over two meetings, STOP here and close in prayer. Inform group members that your next meeting will focus on learning how to love those we don't like.

Start Option: Love I Didn't Deserve (10 Minutes)

Welcome group members as they arrive and suggest they make and wear name tags.

Begin your second meeting by inviting group members to form small groups of no more than six, and share recollections of times someone showed them love that they feel they did not deserve.

Give everyone a few moments to think as you share an incident from your own experience of a time someone was kind or thoughtful or caring to you after you had been less than that to them. Point out that some will find it hard to think of an incident, since repaying evil with good is so rare in our experiences.

After several minutes, invite volunteers to tell the class their experiences. After several have shared, read 1 Peter 3:9 aloud: "Do not repay evil with evil or insult with insult, but with blessing, because to this you were called so that you may inherit a blessing."

Then continue with Step 3 and conclude the session.

Step 3— Learning to Love Those We Don't Even Like (15 Minutes)

Have class members form groups of no more than five or six. Give each group a sheet of newsprint and two or three felt-tip pens. Instruct the groups to make a list of practical tips to help someone begin acting in love towards someone he or she does not like. Tell the groups to make sure their suggestions are specific, and that they are actions they would actually do, not just vague generalities (Be nice), bland platitudes (Try hard) or overworked cliches (Follow the Golden Rule).

After four or five minutes, invite each group to share one or two of their ideas. In each case, ask someone in the group to tell a specific way in which a person could do that action.

Conclude this segment by reading John 13:34 aloud, then add this comment: **As is true throughout Scripture, when God calls us to do something, He always enables us to do that. When we struggle to obey God's call to love others, it is always helpful to remember that such love is not something we "whomp up" on our own initiative. Instead, the love we are called to show to others is the same love we have already received from Christ.**

Option: I Feel Like a Hypocrite

This option will add five minutes to the Step 3 section.

Because of the familiar emphasis on love as a feeling, some people object to the idea of acting in loving ways toward someone they do not like. Present the following guidelines which are helpful in dealing with such objections.

Acting in loving ways in the absence of loving feelings is not hypocritical:

1. Think of all the loving, caring things parents do every day at times (i.e., the middle of the night) when their emotional state is anything but tender affection. The parent does these loving things (feeds the child, changes the diaper, cleans up the mess, etc.) because the child is in need and the parent has committed to care for that child.

2. Faith is often acting in advance of evidence. For example, praising God in the middle of trouble is an act of faith that God's goodness and power are greater than the immediate problem. In the same way, actively seeking God's best even though no tender emotions are present is an act of faith that God can make a positive change in a person's life and in our attitudes.

3. Such actions are also a demonstration of our faith that what we do is because of God's nature and the work He has done in our lives, not because of the lovableness of the other person.

TIP: It does help in such situations to avoid telling persons that we love them. Sometimes people blurt out cliches ("Have a nice day," "It's good to see you") without really thinking about the truth of their words. While it is not necessary or desirable to be bluntly frank ("I'm doing this even though I really don't like you at all"), it is vital to be honest with the person. However, our emotions are really of little or no importance compared with our decision to seek to benefit the person or with our actions toward that purpose.

Step 4 Option—Limits We Try to Impose on God (10 Minutes)

Write on the chalkboard or overhead transparency the following descriptions of God people sometimes use:

- The Man Upstairs
- The Big Dodger in the Sky
- _____ (add your own)

Comment: **These and similar descriptions have been used by some people to refer to God. Their use indicates both a desire to describe God in recognizable human terms and to link God to particular groups or causes.** Invite class members to suggest other examples of ways people sometimes try to define God by our own interests and concerns. As ideas are mentioned, add them to the chalkboard or transparency.

After several people have shared, comment that you are going to look at just one of a great many passages in Scripture which describe God in ways that should stretch our understanding and our faith.

Distribute the five Bible verse sheets you've prepared, giving each one to someone in a different area of the room. Ask each person to stand where everyone can see him or her, unroll the paper and hold it in front of him or her. Then ask the remaining participants to look up Deuteronomy 10:17-21. Walk over to the person holding verse 17 and lead the class in reading that verse aloud, emphasizing the words which are represented by the blank lines. Then ask: **How does this verse stretch our understanding and our faith?** Accept responses, being prepared to point out the surprising last clause: "who shows no partiality and accepts no bribes." Ask: **What does God's impartiality have to do with Him being mighty and awesome?** (Impartiality and fairness are never marks of weakness. They are necessarily linked with God's might, for power which is partial is terrifying to all others. But power which is used fairly is dependable and trustworthy.) Continue similarly with the other four verses, making sure that people see how the descriptions of God in verses 17 and 18 are the basis for the attitudes and actions which should be our responses in verses 19 and 20.

Getting Personal

(10 Minutes)

Remind the class of Deuteronomy 10:21: "He is your praise; he is your God." In light of the truths explored in this session, lead the class in sharing reasons they have for praising God. Ask: **What characteristics and actions of God have you thought of during this session that cause you to respond to Him in praise?**

After several minutes, invite class members to express their praise to God in a time of prayer. Present the following guidelines which can help everyone stay involved and keep the prayer time both informal and fresh:

• Use only informal, conversational language. Avoid "Thee," "Thou," and other stained-glass words and phrases.
• Keep each prayer brief: no more than two or three sentences.
• Address only one topic of praise in any single prayer.
• Before anyone raises a new topic of praise, at least one person should also offer praise for the same thing mentioned in the previous person's prayer.

If your class has more than a dozen people, divide into two or more smaller prayer groups in which people may pray together. Conclude the prayer time by repeating some of the praises mentioned by people, especially those related to God's impartial love.

Getting Personal Option

This option will add five minutes to the Getting Personal section.

Invite class members to stand and form groups of two or three. Ask each person to share with their partners an incident when they failed to show God's impartial, accepting love to someone. Ask the groups to conclude by praying for each other's growth as persons who love God and all of God's people!

Before participants leave announce: **The next session will focus on receiving God's love and forgiveness in our lives.**

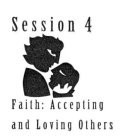
If I Were the Judge

Have you ever wished you could set and impose the penalty for some of life's most aggravating offenses? Work with several other people to compile a list of common, but really irritating, offenses and agree on a penalty for those who commit such violations.

Annoying Offenses   Appropriate Penalties

Love As an Act of Faith

One way of saying it:

> "*Agape* (Christian love) is not an emotional response to someone perceived as being lovable. Instead, it is a pattern of actions intended to help someone become lovable."

What evidence of faith do you see in these statements about love?

- Leviticus 19:18

- Deuteronomy 7:7,8

- John 14:21

- Romans 5:8

- Romans 15:1,2

- 2 Corinthians 5:14,15

- Ephesians 2:4,5

- Colossians 3:12-14

Finish the following statement:

Seeking God's best for a person I don't like is demonstrating my faith that...

Faith: Receiving Love and Forgiveness

Session Keys

Key Verses

"For God so loved the world that he gave his one and only Son, that whoever believes in him shall not perish but have eternal life." John 3:16

"So then, just as you received Christ Jesus as Lord, continue to live in him, rooted and built up in him, strengthened in the faith as you were taught, and overflowing with thankfulness." Colossians 2:6,7

Key Idea

Faith is demonstrated when we receive God's love and forgiveness.

Biblical Basis

Exodus 15:2; Deuteronomy 31:6; Psalm 37:3-5; 119:11; Isaiah 52:13,14; 53:11,12; Matthew 28:1-10; Mark 16:1-14; Luke 24:1-50; John 3:16,17; 20:1-31; Acts 10:39-43; Romans 1:4; 4:7,8; 6:4; 8:28; 10:9,17; 1 Corinthians 15:3-11; 13-19; Galatians 5:6; Colossians 2:6,7; 2 Timothy 2:8; Hebrews 11:1; 1 Peter 1:3-5

Background

Jesus loves me, this I know,

And He died that love to show.

I believe, and that is why,

I have life that will not die.

Most experienced hot air balloon pilots like to fly below the clouds. For them, much of the fun of being up in a balloon is the fresh perspective of what is going on down on the ground. Familiar places and activities take on a whole new appearance.

Faith is like that. Faith in God lets us see life from God's point of view. Faith also lets us see ourselves in light of God's accepting love and forgiveness. Even when we sin, faith allows us to enter God's holy presence, trusting that our confession will bring cleansing, not retribution.

There is another reason balloon pilots like to stay below the clouds. They need to keep their chase car in sight.

When the balloon lands, the pilot and passengers depend on their ground crew to bring them needed supplies and to return them home.

Faith is like that also. Faith keeps God in sight, depending on Him for help, strength, guidance—for everything we need. Faith knows that God will bring us safely home.

Have all of the adults you teach placed their faith in Jesus Christ? Are there people in your class who still need you to guide them to Him? As you prepare for this last lesson of this course, trust God for the opportunity to help at least one person begin the exciting adventure of a life of faith.

Preparation

- Provide blank name tags and felt-tip pens. Make a tag for yourself.
- On a table at the front of the room, provide materials for the Getting Started choice, plus the other activities you choose to offer:
  - **Choice 1: The Question Box**—Cover a large shoebox and lid or a small cardboard box with colorful paper. Draw numerous question marks on the outside of the box. Cut a ½-inch by 3-inch slit in the lid of the box. Cut blank sheets of paper into fourths so that you have one or two pieces for each person in the class. Provide pens or pencils. Place the box on a table at the front of the room with the paper and pencils nearby.
  - **Choice 2: A Resurrection Time Line**—Roll out a 10- to 12-foot length of shelf paper. Draw three solid lines to divide the roll into four equal sections. Using large letters, label the first section "Early Sunday Morning," the second section "During the Day Sunday," the third "Sunday Evening," and the fourth "One Week Later." Provide at least four felt-tip pens. Mount the time line on a wall or bulletin board.
- Write the words from 1 Corinthians 15:14 and 17 on poster board and mount it at the front of the room: "If Christ has not been raised." On two separate sheets of poster board, write the concluding clause from each of those verses: "our preaching is useless and so is your faith" and "your faith is futile; you are still in your sins." Mount these two posters across from each other on the side walls.
- Make two signs from approximately 9x12-inch paper: "Typical Christian" and "Typical Non-Christian."
- Reproduce copies of the "Jesus' Resurrection Brings Hope to All" and "Receiving Love and Forgiveness by Faith" handouts on pages 84-85, providing one copy per person. Have Bibles and pens or pencils for those who need them.
- Option: No Resurrection!?!—Several sheets of newsprints and several felt-tip pens.
- Option: Faith Brings Blessings—In advance enlist two or three people to tell the class in 90 seconds or less how God has blessed their lives as a result of their trust in Christ as Savior.

Session 5 at a Glance

SECTION	ONE-SESSION PLAN		TWO-SESSION PLAN	WHAT YOU'LL DO
Time Schedule	60 to 75 Minutes	More than 75 Minutes	60 Minutes (each session)	
Getting Started	10	10-20	20	Reflect on the Resurrection story
Getting into the Word	40	60-75	40	
Step 1 If Christ Has Not Been Raised	15	25	25	Consider basis for faith in the Resurrection
Step 2 Jesus' Resurrection Brings Hope to All	10	15	15	Compare doubts and responses in the Resurrection narratives
			Session 2 Start Option: 10	
Step 3 Receiving Love and Forgiveness by Faith	15	20	20	Share responses to Jesus' resurrection
(Step 4 Option) Verses Worth Knowing and Believing	(10)	(10-15)	15	Help each other memorize key verses about the Resurrection
Getting Personal	10	10-15	15	A growing faith

Session Plan

Leader's Choice

Two-Meeting Track: This session is designed to be completed in one 60- to 75-minute meeting. If you want to extend the session over two meetings and allow group members more time for discussion, **END** your first meeting and **BEGIN** your second meeting at the stop-and-go symbol in the session plan.

The boxes marked with the clock symbol provide optional learning experiences to extend this session over two meetings or to accommodate a session longer than 60 to 75 minutes.

Getting Started

(10 Minutes)

Choice 1—The Question Box

Welcome group members as they arrive and suggest they make and wear name tags.

Call attention to the Question Box you prepared. Ask each person to take a slip of paper and a pencil and write a question about the Resurrection story as told in the final chapter or two of each of the four Gospels. (Members can refer to their Bibles if they need to jog their memories.) Question slips are then placed inside the box.

After most group members have put a question in the box, ask group members to form groups of no more than six. Distribute the questions evenly among the groups, who will then try to answer them. Allow a minute or two, then ask each group to share one question and one answer of which they are certain and another one of which they are not sure.

After each group has shared, introduce the session topic: **We are going to be exploring the central event on which our Christian faith is based: the resurrection of Jesus. Our goal will be not just that we should all be able to answer questions about the Resurrection, but that we clearly recognize how vital the Resurrection is to the whole fabric of our faith.**

Choice 2—A Resurrection Time Line

Welcome group members as they arrive and suggest they make and wear name tags.

Call attention to the time line you have prepared. Explain that they will have three or four minutes to see how many resurrection appearances of Jesus they can place on the time line. Encourage group members to work in groups, with some groups looking at Matthew 28:1-10, while other groups check Mark 16:1-14, Luke 24, or John 20.

Call time after a few minutes and invite volunteers to tell what happened in each of the four time periods listed. Their answers should include:

- Early Sunday Morning—Women discovered the tomb open and empty, saw the angel; Jesus appeared to Mary Magdalene; Peter and John run to the tomb;
- During the Day Sunday—Jesus appeared to Peter and to travelers on the road to Emmaus;
- Sunday Evening—Jesus appeared to group of disciples in the Upper Room
- One Week Later—Jesus appeared to disciples and Thomas.

After the time line has been explained (and corrected, if necessary) introduce the session topic: **We are going to be exploring the central event on which our Christian faith is based—the resurrection of Jesus. Our goal will not be that we** should know the sequence of events surrounding the Resurrection, but that we clearly recognize how vital the Resurrection is to the whole fabric of our faith.

Getting Started Option: Eyewitness News

This option will add 10 minutes to the Getting Started section.

Point out: For many years after Jesus' resurrection, everyone who had witnessed one of His appearances must have told their story to everyone they could get to listen. We should not be surprised that the resurrection is one of the few events in Jesus' life that is given detailed attention in all four Gospels. Nor is there any reason to wonder that Paul—who clearly was not on the scene at the time—should pass on the stories that he had been told by others.

Ask everyone to turn to 1 Corinthians 15:3-11. Ask a class member to read these verses aloud. Explain that the reader will pause after each verse so you can insert brief explanatory comments:

Verse 3—Paul is passing on information he received from others. He is scrupulously honest to not take credit for having seen something when he wasn't there. In the ancient world, passing on stories and traditions was a much more accurate process than today when people have learned to depend on written notes instead of training themselves to listen and remember.

Verse 4—From that amazing day when Jesus explained the Scriptures about Himself to those grieving disciples on the Emmaus road, the Church had focused on the fact that Jesus' death, burial, and resurrection fulfilled a host of announcements written hundreds of years before.

Verse 5—These appearances of Jesus are mentioned in both Luke and John.

Verse 6—This big crowd was probably present in Matthew 28:16-20.

Verse 7—This James was the half brother of Jesus, who was not one of the apostles. He did not believe until after the Resurrection.

Verse 8—Paul met Jesus in a vision on the road to Damascus, probably several years after the Resurrection.

Verse 9—Anyone who doubts the validity of Paul's encounter has to explain the dramatic transformation of this enemy of the faith.

Verse 10—Still Paul claims no special credit or status. Along with the rest of us, he benefited from the grace of God.

Verse 11—What a summary! No matter who the messenger, the message was the same, and it is the foundation of our faith: Jesus Christ was raised from the dead!

Getting into the Word

(40 Minutes)

Step 1—If Christ Has Not Been Raised (15 Minutes)

Introduce this topic by directing attention to the poster with the phrase Paul repeated in 1 Corinthians 15: "If Christ Has Not Been Raised."

Lead the class members in reading the phrase in unison to emphasize the importance Paul placed on our understanding of the impact of the Resurrection. Then point out the two posters on the side walls. Lead the class in reading the first phrase in unison again, followed by half the class reading together from the poster on their side of the room. Again, everyone reads aloud from the front poster, and the other half of the class reads together from the poster on their side. If the class is a little slow or reluctant to get into the rhythm and spirit of this group reading, repeat it once or twice. Even if they catch on the first time, repeat it just for emphasis.

Ask everyone to silently read 1 Corinthians 15:13-19. Then ask: **Why does Paul "put all his eggs in one basket" this way? Why does he place such supreme importance on this one historical event?** Encourage group members to respond, and be prepared to add the following comments if necessary for clarification:

1. The Resurrection was the proof that Jesus was truly God's Son, not an ordinary human. If He was not raised, then He was either deluded or deceitful in what He had taught about Himself before His arrest.

2. The Resurrection was also the completion of Jesus' sacrificial death on our behalf. Without the Resurrection's demonstration of God's power and approval, Jesus would have been merely another martyr who died for a cause, not the Savior of the world whose death brings cleansing and forgiveness. Jesus himself had said that anyone who did not believe in Him "will indeed die in your sins" (John 8:24).

3. The bottom line: Christianity with no resurrection is either delusions, myths or lies. There may be a measure of inspiration in the stories about Jesus, but without the Resurrection there is no power to transform our lives.

4. Paul clearly shows that the Resurrection is our only valid reason for holding on to

a belief in life after death. With no resurrection, the hope of heaven is merely wishful thinking based on fabrications.

After a few minutes of interaction, ask: **Why did Paul say that Christians "are to be pitied" (1 Corinthians 15:19) if we have no valid hope beyond this life?** (The struggles and persecution endured by vast numbers of Christians would simply be a cruel joke if this life were all there is. Even those Christians who have not overtly suffered would be the victims of a bitter hoax, living lives chasing a lie and so missing the opportunity to live for the moment.)

Ask for two volunteers to come to the front of the room. Assign one to be a "typical Christian" and the other to be a "typical non-Christian." Give each one the appropriate sign you prepared. Ask them to stand in front of the class, each holding their sign. Explain to the class that this typical non-Christian knows nothing about the Resurrection other than it was religious and had something to do with Easter and rabbits. The typical Christian is trying to explain why this event of nearly 2,000 years ago is important for both of them today.

Ask the class to suggest clear, simple, non-jargon explanations the typical Christian can give. As one is suggested, the typical Christian turns to the typical non-Christian and gives that explanation. Of course, the non-Christian will not understand and for clarification must ask a question (e.g. "What do you mean the Resurrection could make a difference in my life?"). This gives the class the opportunity to suggest an answer, and the interaction continues. You may need to be ready to offer an example or two to help group members get started thinking of non-cliché ways in which Jesus' resurrection is of vital importance today.

Summarize this segment by reading aloud Paul's words in 2 Timothy 2:8: "Remember Jesus Christ, raised from the dead, descended from David. This is my gospel."

Option: No Resurrection!?!

This option will add 10 minutes to the Step 1 section.

Divide class into groups of no more than five or six per group. Give each group a sheet of newsprint and three or four felt-tip pens. Then comment: **It's one thing to talk about the implications if Jesus had not risen from the dead. It's another thing to push ourselves to feel and visualize the real impact on our lives if there had not been a resurrection.**

Instruct each group to sketch a poster showing one or more ways in which our lives would be different if Jesus had remained in the tomb. Suggest possible themes the groups could use: the Church, an individual, a marriage, the future, etc. Explain that they will have five minutes in which to work, so their artwork should be very quick and avoid lots of detail. As a poster, the message and graphics should be clear from across the room.

Some group members will probably mumble that they can't draw or that they don't like "artsy" activities. Ask them to be good sports for the benefit of others in the class who put up with all the discussion and study approaches which have been the bulk of this course. Besides, approaching a familiar topic in a different way is a very useful means of gaining fresh perspective.

After five minutes, invite each group to show and explain their poster.

Step 2—Jesus' Resurrection Brings Hope to All (10 Minutes)

Divide class into at least four groups of no more than five or six each, distribute the "Jesus' Resurrection Brings Hope to All" handouts. Assign each of the groups one of Jesus' appearances listed on the page (Luke 24:1-12—the women and Peter; Luke 24:13-33—the road to Emmaus; John 20:10-18—Mary Magdalene; John 20:19-31—the disciples and Thomas). Instruct the groups to read their passages, then work together to answer the questions on the page:

1. No one in any of the resurrection narratives had expected Jesus to return to life. All had doubts and questions. What might have been the causes of the doubts?
2. What made the difference in moving from doubt to faith?
3. What was the response when doubt and uncertainty were replaced by faith?
4. Based on what you read in these verses, what do you see as the greatest benefit these early believers gained from Jesus' resurrection?

Other than question 3, the answers to the questions are not explicitly stated in the passages. Class members will need to read thoughtfully, then compare insights about the significance of what they read.

NOTE: You might need to caution your class about this approach to a passage. While trying to flesh out the people and incidents beyond the limits of the narrative can be very helpful in making a passage come to life (the reason for doing it), no one should claim that any judgment they make is conclusive unless it is clearly stated in the passage. There is sometimes an uneasy balance that the thoughtful reader must strike in reading a passage and making its meaning personal. A good rule of thumb is to keep returning to the words of the passage and asking, "Where do you see that idea in these verses?"

After four or five minutes, invite volunteers from each group to share their answers to the questions. Move as quickly as possible through the first three questions in order to allow adequate time for as many group members as possible to share what they see as the greatest benefit group members gain from Jesus' resurrection. The more group members who share their insights, the greater will be the impact and understanding.

Option: Old Testament Prophecies and Jesus' Death and Resurrection

This option will add five minutes to the Step 2 section.

The Luke 24 passage mentions Peter's visit to the tomb only briefly. Read aloud John 20:1-9 which recounts Peter and John's run to the tomb in more detail. Reread verse 9 which refers to Peter and John's lack of understanding of what the Scriptures said about Christ's victory over death. A similar lack is central to the story of Jesus'

encounter on the road to Emmaus (Luke 24:25-27). Ask: **Why is it important for us to see the link between Old Testament prophecies and Jesus' death and resurrection?** (Jesus' fulfillment of the prophecies not only is the continuation and expansion of God's eternal plan for Israel and all of humanity, it is also the validation of Jesus' identity as the Messiah. See Romans 1:4.) Ask for volunteers to read aloud the following two Old Testament prophecies which refer to Christ's suffering and glory:

• Isaiah 52:13,14
• Isaiah 53:11,12

Note: If you are completing this session in one meeting, ignore this break and continue with Step 3.

Two-Meeting Track: If you want to spread this session over two meetings, STOP here and close in prayer. Inform group members that your next meeting will focus on learning how to love those we don't like.

Start Option: A Time to Share (10 Minutes)

Welcome group members as they arrive and suggest they make and wear name tags.

Begin your final meeting by inviting group members to form groups of no more than five group members and share with each other one or two ways in which these sessions on faith have been helpful. If time permits, take two or three minutes to invite volunteers to share with the whole class what they had just told their small group.

Then continue with Step 3 and conclude the session.

Step 3—Receiving Love and Forgiveness by Faith (15 Minutes)

Distribute a copy of the "Receiving Love and Forgiveness by Faith" handout to each member. Instruct them to select one of the four passages printed on the page and read about these benefits which are made available to us because of Jesus' death and resurrection. Then each person is to write a brief paragraph describing what he or she is doing or intends to do to be certain of gaining those benefits. Assure members they will not be required to share their paragraphs with anyone. Allow up to five minutes for group members to read and write.

Take each Scripture in sequence and invite volunteers to suggest possible actions people can take to receive the benefits in the verses. Some may want to read aloud the paragraphs they wrote. Others will prefer to share more general answers.

Somewhere in this process, it should start to become obvious that the necessary actions are the same for all these benefits. Point out that God's "benefits package" is better than a two-for-one or even a four-for-one deal. All we need to do is believe in Jesus Christ, to actively and obediently put our trust in Him to make us right with God, and then God begins to shower us with blessings in abundant measure.

Share from your own experience how your trust in Christ has brought you one or more of the benefits God promises. This does not need to be a dramatic "rescued from disaster" story. Simply tell of one benefit you have received from faith in Christ.

Option: Faith Brings Blessings

This option will add five minutes to the Step 3 section.

Ask the members you enlisted before class to share ways in which God has blessed their lives as a result of their trust in Christ as Savior. You may want to invite others to share similarly.

Step 4 Option: Verses Worth Knowing and Believing (10 Minutes)

Write the following references on the chalkboard or overhead transparency. Add others from this course which have been significant to your class.

- Exodus 15:2
- Deuteronomy 31:6
- Psalm 37:3-5
- John 3:16,17
- Romans 4:7,8
- Romans 8:28
- Romans 10:9
- Galatians 5:6
- Hebrews 11:1
- 1 Peter 1:3-5

Begin this segment by reading aloud Romans 10:17: **"Consequently, faith comes from hearing the message, and the message is heard through the word of Christ."** Add this comment: **In our journey to learn more about faith and to see our faith in God grow, we have looked at various passages of Scripture dealing with the topic. To ensure that we remember some of the key truths we've explored, we're going to work together for a few minutes to memorize some key verses about faith.**

If some of your class members feel they are no good at memorizing or too old to succeed, offer these added comments: **The psalmist who reflected on hiding God's word in his heart (see Psalm 119:11) was not merely looking back on childhood learning experiences. He is describing an ongoing, active involvement in reading, learning, loving and obeying the Scriptures.**

Instruct group members to select a partner or two, with each one choosing one or more verses to memorize in the next few minutes. Offer these tips to aid in memorizing:

- If the passage has several phrases, clauses or sentences, learn the last phrase first, then add the preceding ones to it, one at a time until you reach the beginning. Most people remember the opening words of verses and songs, but tend to get muddled the further in they go. By learning the last section first you ensure that each time you review it, you'll be going over those last sections repeatedly, making it easier to remember them later.
- Write the verse on blank paper or an index card, one phrase per line. Read the verse to yourself, taking turns covering a different line each time. It usually only takes a few tries before you can say the whole verse without looking at any of the lines.

- As soon as you think you can say most of the passage, say it aloud to a friend who can prompt you if you get stuck. Saying the verse orally as well as mentally adds to your memorizing efficiency.

Allow five or six minutes for everyone to work, then invite volunteers to say their verses aloud to the class. Be sure you have memorized a verse to share, as well.

Getting Personal

(10 Minutes)

Ask class members to return to groups of no more than five or six each. Instruct each person to share his or her answer to *one* of the following three questions with his or her small group:

1. **One way I have seen my faith grow in the past few weeks is...**
2. **One way I continue to struggle with my faith is...**
3. **One way in which I plan to continue helping my faith grow stronger is...**

Remind the class that faith is not a constant like a rock which rarely if ever changes. Instead, faith is a living, growing entity which must be nurtured and exercised or it will wither.

Getting Personal Option: Give Thanks

This option will add five minutes to the Getting Personal section.

Ask the class to stand and join hands. Lead the class in a closing time of one-sentence prayers of thanks for insights gained and for faith that is growing.

Dismiss the session with a brief closing prayer.

Jesus' Resurrection Brings Hope to All

The Women & Peter (Luke 24:1-12)	Mary Magdalene (John 20:10-18)
The Road to Emmaus (Luke 24:13-33)	The Disciples and Thomas (John 20:19-31)

1. No one in any of the Resurrection narratives had expected Jesus to return to life. All had doubts and questions. What might have been the causes of the doubts?

2. What made the difference in moving from doubt to faith?

Jesus' Resurrection Brings Hope to All

3. What was the response when doubt and uncertainty was replaced by faith?

4. Based on what you read in these verses, what do you see as the greatest benefit these early believers gained from Jesus' resurrection?

Receiving Love and Forgiveness by Faith

Benefits of the Resurrection	How Can I Receive Them?
"They killed him by hanging him on a tree, but God raised him from the dead on the third day and caused him to be seen. All the prophets testify about him that everyone who believes in him receives forgiveness of sins through his name" (Acts 10:39,43).	
"We were therefore buried with him through baptism into death in order that, just as Christ was raised from the dead through the glory of the Father, we too may live a new life" (Romans 6:4).	
"Praise be to the God and Father of our Lord Jesus Christ! In his great mercy he has given us new birth into a living hope through the resurrection of Jesus Christ from the dead, and into an inheritance that can never perish, spoil or fade—kept in heaven for you, who through faith are shielded by God's power until the coming of the salvation that is ready to be revealed in the last time" (1 Peter 1:3-5).	
"For God so loved the world that he gave his one and only Son, that whoever believes in him shall not perish but have eternal life. For God did not send his Son into the world to condemn the world, but to save the world through him" (John 3:16,17).	

Teach the Whole Bible at a Fraction of the Price

Continue your journey through the Bible and save some money along the way.

Here's a coupon for $2.00 off your purchase of the **What the Bible Is All About 102 Old Testament: Job—Malachi Group Study Guide!** There are 4 books in the entire series, so be on the look-out for your coupon as you begin your New Testament studies next quarter!

You've made it half way through the Old Testament, here's an incentive to help you make it all the way through.

Look for the other volumes of the *What the Bible Is All About 101* series:

What the Bible Is All About 102 Old Testament: Job—Malachi Group Study Guide

What the Bible Is All About 201 New Testament: Matthew—Philippians Group Study Guide

What the Bible Is All About 202 New Testament: Colossians—Revelation Group Study Guide

---

$2 off

Simply fill out this coupon, sign and return it to your favorite retailer and you'll receive $2 off the purchase price of **What the Bible Is All About 102 Old Testament: Job—Malachi Group Study Guide** (ISBN 08307.17978).

Name_____

Address _____

City _____ State_____ Zip _____

Phone_____

Signature _____
(required for redemption)

Gospel Light